Home Away from Home

LifeWays Care of
Children and Families

Cynthia Aldinger
and Mary O'Connell

*We dedicate this book to our husbands, Michael and Jim,
for their tireless and generous support; and to our children
for teaching us how to be mothers and caregivers.*

Acknowledgments

THE STORY OF LIFEWAYS that you hold in your hands was made possible through the help of many inspiring individuals, some of whom we would like to acknowledge here.

Many thanks to Rahima Baldwin Dancy for her editorial and collegial support, Joan Almon for her tireless work for the protection of childhood and for writing the Foreword of this book, and Ruth Ann Ball for her much-appreciated perspective as a scholar of Early Childhood Education.

We have many talented souls as part of our LifeWays family. We would particularly like to acknowledge Valerie Valentine, LifeWays Milwaukee parent, for copy editing; Chelsea Cloeter, former parent of LifeWays Lake Country, for book design; and Shelby Downing, East Coast LifeWays training graduate, for the beautiful photos that grace the front and back covers of the book.

Our deepest gratitude is extended to the LifeWays caregivers who shared their stories for this book: Susan Silverio, Faith Baldwin, Marcy Andrew, Margo Running, Jacqueline Beecher, Jess Henry, and Ginger Georger. And we thank their exemplary teachers and mentors in our training centers.

We would like to acknowledge the wise women with whom we serve on the LifeWays North America board—Marianne Alsop, Rosario Villasana-Ruiz, Trisha Lambert, Susan Silverio, and Rahima Baldwin Dancy—for supporting and advising us throughout the process of creating *Home Away from Home* and for all they do to carry on the work of LifeWays. Thank you also to Lori Barian, who wrote the initial grant request to get us started, and to the Rudolf Steiner Foundation, which answered that request.

And, finally, last but certainly not least, we thank the many parents, children, and caregivers who create the community that is LifeWays. We are so very grateful.

With love and appreciation,
Cynthia and Mary

Contents

Foreword

WHEN I BEGAN teaching young children in 1971, there was little need for child care. Most mothers were at home, or if not, then a close family member cared for the children. But gradually the need for child care grew; and while I visited some fine centers, especially in Scandinavia, many that I visited in the U.S. lacked the basic warmth and beauty that children desperately need to blossom and grow.

I often wondered how a typical center could possibly build relationships when the children were divided by ages and assigned to a new caregiver every year. In addition, providing care is intense work that is vastly underpaid; the rate of attrition among typical child care workers is shockingly high. Home-based care provided a potential solution but too often seemed to be of poor quality.

I was involved with Waldorf early education in those years but not with child care directly, so my concerns remained a bit abstract. Then one fall I visited a Waldorf kindergarten in New England. Among the robust, playful children was a little girl who seemed unusually thin and wan. When I asked about her, the teacher explained that she had been in a standard child care setting from infancy until she entered the Waldorf school a month before. I knew that this was not a child living in poverty with a shortage of food, but she reminded me of a little chicken that had been plucked of its surrounding feathers. She seemed so cold and bare. Her image haunted me.

I stayed in touch with her teacher and was gratified to learn that she responded to the warmth of the classroom—in particular to the teacher's own warmth as well as to a sheepskin-lined basket that the child adopted as her nest. After a few months her feathers grew back and she filled out.

Although I was only with her for a morning, she had found her way into my heart and awakened the question in me: What could we do about child care? I visited Waldorf child care centers in Denmark and Holland and was amazed at the health and vitality of the children, although they spent long hours away from home every day from infancy onward.

We began to have conversations about child care in the board meetings of the Waldorf Early Childhood Association (WECAN), a board on which Cynthia Aldinger and I both served. I was so grateful that Cynthia, Rena Osmer, and a few others felt strongly called to develop child care programs. They wrestled with ideals as well as practical issues. Cynthia's passion and her knowledge grew over time, and I recall one meeting where we said to her with some firmness: We believe you that it is possible. Now show us. Do it!

A year or two later we were invited to meet at the first LifeWays center. That was a magical meeting. Cynthia's dream now stood in the world, and we rejoiced for her and all the families she was serving. The center spoke to my longing that somehow here in the U.S., without benefit of the financial subsidies child care centers receive in other countries, there could be a program that allowed children to grow with warmth and good care.

I still recall that visit vividly. The suites were homelike with separate rooms for different activities, and each housed a mixed-age group from infants to kindergartners. They had the air of well-tended homes—modest but beautiful. Best of all was the care provided by loving adults.

The quality of care was confirmed for me when I watched two little four-year-old girls tending their dolls with the same tender gestures as their caregivers gave the infants and toddlers. I began to see the lasting power of LifeWays. I had often wondered how children in child care, surrounded only by children their own age, would ever learn to care for others. Here, in these mixed-age groupings, the traditional imitation of care typically experienced in a family with several children was taking place.

I am delighted that this book now exists and describes the LifeWays approach in such a living way. The content ranges from the moving descriptions of "Marie's" beautiful home care to the legal and business questions of running a center. It even includes tips for advocating for change in child care.

To Mary O'Connell and Cynthia Aldinger I can only say thank you. You

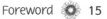

have done a great service to caregivers and parents, but also to all those who serve children and care for them—grandparents, godparents, babysitters, friends, and relatives. Anyone who has cared for a young child for a few hours, a few days, or through the years of childhood has experienced the joys and challenges described in this book. To be invited into your world and to learn from your experiences is a privilege.

This book also relates to my current work with the Alliance for Childhood. It was founded eleven years ago because many of us in education and health care saw a troubling decline in children's health and well-being. Children showed signs of stress and worry, and this was affecting their physical and mental health. We wanted to work on behalf of all children, and we wanted to protect and preserve childhood itself as a time of enormous capacity but also of great vulnerability.

One of the first things the Alliance did was to identify the "healthy essentials" of childhood. Children need food, clothing, and shelter to physically survive; but there are other essentials they need to grow and thrive. Among these are play, the arts, language, handwork, a relationship with nature, a sense of the sacred, and, most central of all, relationships with caring adults. What I love about LifeWays is that it honors and cultivates all these essentials, and also places at the heart of its approach the child's relationship with caring adults.

We need a revolution in child care in this country. This book can help fuel it.

—Joan Almon
Executive Director
U.S. Alliance for Childhood

Introduction

My hunch is that if we allow ourselves to give who we really are to the children in our care, we will some way inspire cartwheels in their hearts.

—Fred Rogers

PARTICIPATING in the growing, changing life of a child is one of the great privileges in life. Yes, they are our heart medicine, our joy and delight; and they can also bring us to our knees as we pray for the wisdom to know how to meet their energy. Whether a child is quiet, inward, and pensive or robust, outgoing, and wild, we often find ourselves in a land of mystery regarding how to support him. As our LifeWays trainings have expanded, we have more and more parents enrolling alongside child care providers, preschool teachers, nannies, and parent educators. One thing we all eventually come to learn: The child is our main textbook, and we are his main curriculum!

Studying human development certainly helps to unveil some of the mysteries of what it is to be a child and what it means to be an adult worthy of being imitated by children. We are exceedingly grateful for the insightful revelations offered by Dr. Rudolf Steiner, the founder of the Waldorf school movement, and other child development experts who offer the understanding that simple living is what the child needs most.

This book is not primarily on child development, however. Soon we will introduce you to an innovative approach to caring for children that supports their natural stages of development. Childhood is not about preparation for adulthood. Of course, every stage we are in as growing human beings is, in some way, preparing us for the next stage; but that happens by design, not

by curriculum. We hold childhood as a sacred foundation upon which all of the rest of life is built. If we want that foundation to be rich, strong, and sustainable, then we do not want to cut corners by shortening the length of time a person spends building that foundation. Fast-forwarding a person through childhood in order to reach some ultimate goal called adulthood seems absurd at best. Many hold sacred the words in the book of Matthew: "Except you become as a little child, you cannot enter the kingdom of Heaven." Yet many early childhood curricula urge children toward premature adulthood.

A recent best seller for adults is *The Power of Now,* by Eckhart Tolle. The main quality that he writes about is that of being "present." In fact, there are several books on the market about "presence," and a relatively new word has been created called *presencing,* which means "the act of being present." Guess what young children do all the time? They live in the present moment.

LifeWays was developed to support the possibility for young children to fully penetrate their presence in noninstitutional environments that look, act, and feel as homelike as possible. As a little child in a LifeWays center in Vancouver, British Columbia, said, "I know all about life because I go to Life-Ways." As a matter of fact, that is exactly what we had in mind when we began exploring the idea back in 1997.

Now, by offering this *how-to* book on establishing LifeWays child care homes and centers and parent-child programs, it is our greatest hope that many of you will find the confidence to open a LifeWays program yourself. The children need you. The families need you. And the culture at large needs you. For those who do not intend to open child care or parent support programs but are instead seeking inspiration for your primary responsibility— parenting—we hope you will be inspired by the ideals, principles, and practices revealed in these pages.

When we started the first LifeWays project in Wisconsin, we began navigating the world of rules and regulations that felt so far away from the imagination we were carrying. If helping children and families experience health-giving, nurturing care was the original impulse, was it appropriate to spend our time fighting bureaucratic dragons that could completely derail the original inspiration?

Thank the stars in heaven for Mary O'Connell and thanks for the guiding light of destiny that brought us together and into the formative work of LifeWays North America. While loving, appreciating, and living the ideals and principles upon which LifeWays child care is built and deeply respecting the view of child development that stands behind it, Mary also brings clarity and well-grounded experience to navigating the regulatory world that is currently obligatory in the field of child care.

Mary's chapters on regulatory bodies and on business questions are very helpful for those of you ready to take up the cause of making this innovative child care available to more people. We need your help, and building strong early childhood programs that will be sustainable is one way you can make a difference. If you find yourself drawn toward the political scene and desire to take up the cause of making changes that support practical, common sense, healthy practices in child care, please read the short section on advocacy at the end of the book.

Now please enter Chapter 1 as if entering a LifeWays home away from home for children and families. We welcome you to make yourself comfortable, relax, and enjoy.

—*Cynthia Aldinger*
January 2010

What Is LifeWays Child Care?

BY CYNTHIA ALDINGER

Children need people to respect, adults whose example and loving authority they follow. They need a range of experience—tenderness and kindness, boldness and courage, even mischief and misbehavior. Children need to be introduced to a life of principles, and given the freedom to discover their own.

—Alliance for Childhood

RECENTLY A COLLEAGUE introduced me to the concept behind a trim tab, which is a small device that can be used to turn a large boat in an emergency situation when it might take too long to correct the main steering mechanism, the rudder. In a turbulent storm, one can be thankful that such a device exists. Perhaps this characterizes what LifeWays is trying to accomplish on behalf of children and families everywhere.

LifeWays child care is first and foremost based on the intention to deinstitutionalize the care of young children in child care centers and homes. Recognizing that the fundamental needs of the child are met through daily life activities and healthy relationships, LifeWays has set about to radically change the direction organized child care has taken over the past few decades.

There are a variety of models of LifeWays care, some of which will be described in the next chapter. Some offer all-day care, and others offer part

day. Some are in homes and others are in centers. They are all, however, based on the *living arts* that you will read about in this chapter. These *living arts* (*domestic activity, nurturing care, creative discovery, and social ability*) can be applied in a child care home or in a LifeWays center with multiple groups of mixed-age children, where the environment is as homelike as possible.

At the end of this chapter you can read more about LifeWays principles and practices. There is even a "quiz" you can take to see how many principles and practices you can identify in the following story. There are also several text boxes in this chapter exploring the *whys and wherefores* of some of the experiences at Marie's LifeWays home.

Marie's is not an actual place, but it is a real story. The story represents an amalgamation of experiences I have had over the years visiting LifeWays homes and centers. It represents numerous wonderful caregivers, children, and parents; and I hope it represents a life that some of you, the readers, will become inspired to emulate. We need more homes and centers to offer life-based, simplicity-based, wonder-based care; a level of care that inspires a sense of goodness in the world for our young children; a sense of calm support for our families; and the joy of lifelong learning for our children, caregivers, and teachers.

Marie's is a home model with one full-time caregiver, two part-time caregivers, and eight children from infancy to six years old. Marie is there full-time with a long midday break, and Stefan and Charelle are both part-time. Stefan has his own work in the afternoons and weekends teaching yoga, and Charelle is currently a student. I represent the "adopted" grandma, who helps out once a week for a few hours; I highly recommend that caregivers find support people like that, people who develop relationships with the children and can provide other sets of helping hands. For years Marie worked by herself with six children. Only recently did she decide to hire two people to work with her, one mornings and the other afternoons. This offers her the flexibility to have a longer break in the afternoon and to take days off. It is also her way of handing down a legacy of hope that more people will choose to enter this field of work. Recently she found a promising property and plans to open a three-suite child care center within the next few years!

Come with me now to a day at Marie's LifeWays home. . . .

The Day Begins

Coming in through the back door, I can see Marie at the changing table with a sweet butterball baby, and Stefan is at the dining-room table chopping vegetables. Several children are at the table with him, and occasionally I hear a wave of laughter. He is singing the song "Vegetable Soup," and the children crack up every time he sings, "Hello, Ms. Potato, I dig you, I do!" A couple of children are playing in the living room, although I cannot see them because they have created a tent under the coffee table and are having a giggling good time.

I enter with as little fanfare as possible and quietly go over to Marie to give a hug and gaze for a moment at the baby.

"Good morning," I softly sing out.

"Oh, good morning. Welcome!" She smiles. "How is your new grandbaby?"

"Pure heaven and total perfection!" I grin. "What more can I say?!"

"Well, congratulations, Grandma!"

I step back and quietly watch Marie sing a little touching-game song to the baby before she oils him and finishes with his diaper. He responds with a Mississippi-wide grin. Marie tends to him without any sense of rush and with a deep regard for giving him time to respond to her as she gets him dressed.

Here's your little foot
And here's your little toes;
Now into your sock
Your little foot goes.

He slowly lifts his foot in response. Once he is fully dressed, she holds out her hands, and he puffs out his chest as indication that he is ready to be picked up. He snuggles into her soft, flowing tunic top. Marie always dresses in a way that even her clothing is like a personal invitation to the children for cuddles.

"I really like his cap," I say.

"And how about this?!" She grins and shows me his undershirt and leggings. "We did a fund-raiser to purchase caps, undershirts, and leggings— enough for the parents of the infants and toddlers to have a set at home and for us to have spares here. When a baby outgrows them, the parents bring them back to us. These are made so well, they last for years."

"Wow! That's great." I am delighted. I give the baby a little nuzzle and head over to the couch, giving a wave to Stefan, who greets me with his eyes and finishes his chopping. I admire his cooking apron. It looks like something a chef would wear. The children put the sliced carrots on a plate and the rest of the veggies into the soup pot. The leftover bits and pieces are scraped into the compost bucket. A toddler is sitting on the kitchen floor playing with a pot and a wooden spoon.

Settling onto the couch, I pull out my yarn to work on the hotpads I am crocheting for Marie's table. Sasha toddles over and hands me a book. "Gook!" she says. "Is that for 'book' or 'look'?" I wonder. She crawls up into my lap, and I tuck away my crochet for a while. A few nursery rhymes later, she becomes more interested in the shrieking of three children playing house in the corner. Five-year-old Samuel is tossing clothespins into the playhouse until encouraged by Stefan to accompany him out into the garden to plant some flowers. Samuel asks if his friend, an almost-five-year-old, can come too; and his complaining shifts to joy of camaraderie as they clean up the clothespins and then go outside to do some real work!

I am filled with gratitude that Stefan finds meaning and purpose in working with young children, and for one fleeting moment I wonder if cloning would really be such a bad thing! Imagine having a young man like this one in every child care setting! Of course, I am kidding about the cloning, but not about my desire for more men to enter the field of child care.

Sasha returns to me, and we play a bouncing game that thoroughly delights her as she squeals for more.

> *Father and Mother and Uncle John went a riding one by one.*
> *Father fell off—Plop!*
> *Mother fell off—Plop!*
> *But Uncle John went on and on and on and on and on—*
> *Whoopsie!*

Three more times and that's my limit. Grandmas have some privileges, such as saying when enough is enough!

Marie makes a phone call to the parent of a new child to see when she might visit with her at home. The home visit was something Marie found made her work easier, strengthening the bridge between the child's home and

her home. Once the parents realized that she was not there to "inspect" them, they relaxed, and the children loved showing her their bedrooms and their favorite things. Children would often talk about this visit for weeks, sometimes months, afterward. "Remember when you came to my house and . . ."

After she finishes her call, Marie brings in a load of fresh laundry. She gets some paper and crayons for two of the children, puts a king-sized sheet over the dining table for some children to play under, and then sits at her desk to make out her grocery list.

One of the children fusses that she's tired. I encourage her to get me a drink of water and get one for herself also. Cups and a small pitcher of water are always accessible to encourage everyone to drink throughout the day. She brings me a cup of water, after taking a swig out of it herself, and then sits on the couch, contemplatively studying a painting on the living-room wall. It is a painting of a ship sailing off to sea, and standing on the shore is a couple with their arms wrapped around each other. "Well, I guess they just got left behind," she surmises. Then she points to another painting of a beautiful woman holding an infant in her arms and proclaims, "That's me and my mommy when I was a baby." She picks up a doll and puts it under her shirt to nurse it and quietly starts humming.

I start sorting and folding the laundry and another child comes over to help. "Let's find all the red napkins first!" she says enthusiastically. We get all the napkins sorted by color before we start folding. It is clear to me that she has done this many times, as her folding skills impress me.

Notes of Interest

How does Marie's home-based model differ from a center-based model?

Of course, the obvious difference is that Marie and her colleagues are in an actual home, so less needs to be done to make it look and feel like a home. It already is. Ideally, in a center-based model, each group of children and caregivers functions in a very similar fashion to how Marie and her staff function. It is the physical space that will vary the most.

Our pilot LifeWays center was in a site with three groups of caregivers and children. We were quite fortunate that each group had more than one room, including a dedicated sleeping room and a small dining area, as well as their own bathroom. The three groups shared a central kitchen. We referred to each of these groups as a LifeWays *suite*, and our business manager enjoyed saying that LifeWays child care was *home suite home!* Such an ideal setup cannot always be replicated for a child care center. You can read about how others have worked with their space to make it as homelike as possible. Another difference in a child care center as compared to a home is that multiple groups function as a little neighborhood, visiting one another, playing outside together, and celebrating together. Just as children in earlier times could go next door or across the street to visit friends, in LifeWays centers they may just be traveling across the hallway!

What's all the excitement about the infant's cap and underwear?

Because children easily lose heat through their heads, feet, and mid-section, we encourage parents and caregivers to keep these parts of chil-

dren's bodies protected; and the caps and undergarments do this. Wool or silk-wool blend is helpful in almost all seasons because it breathes well and wicks away moisture. In warmer seasons, cotton is fine; however, when a child gets sweaty, cotton gets damp and can cause chilling. When children are kept appropriately warm, it aids in their digestion, their behavior, and their general well-being. Young children

typically do not have a developed sense of body temperature. When a young child complains and wants to take off her coat, it is rarely because she is hot; more likely, she feels encumbered by outerwear. It is up to the adult to enforce keeping the child appropriately dressed and helping her cope with wearing her outerwear. A good way to determine if a child is warm enough is to check hands, feet, and tummy. If they are cool, the child probably needs another layer. If the child is sweaty or clammy, however, she may be overdressed. Regardless of the temperature, it is helpful to keep an infant's head covered most of the time, particularly until the fontanel is closed. As sensitive as young children are to all the sensory impressions they encounter each day, this extra layer of protection helps to keep them from becoming overstimulated.

Why is the food being prepared and the laundry being tended to while the children are there?

LifeWays child care is based primarily on the living arts, as mentioned above and which you can read about in the section on principles and practices. Many children have limited exposure to the practical activities of a household. Experiencing and participating in *everyday-life* activities help to provide a solid foundation of skills and capacities.

Is there a specific approach to discipline used in LifeWays child care?

LifeWays uses an approach to discipline based on a variety of tools for guiding a child and strengthening the caregiver. Samuel's behavior has been difficult at times. Two years ago, Marie had even considered whether or not they could continue to have him in their care. When they met about the possibility of letting him go, however, they all agreed that there were things they could do to support him. Stefan was particularly keen on working with him. Through their efforts to meet his energy and a close partnership with his parents, they were able to hold on to him and experience the joy of seeing him grow.

Most conventional child care programs have learning centers to focus the children's play and learning experience. How does this work in LifeWays?

As you read further, you will discover that at LifeWays, *life* is the curriculum. The whole environment might be considered the center of learning. However, you can also discern that at Marie's certain things happen in particular places. Food preparation, eating, and learning table manners all happen in the kitchen/dining area. Tending to the laundry is always done in the same area. Experiencing nature and all the basic science that nature introduces happens outside in the play yard and on the nature walks, along with large motor skills such as climbing, jumping, and running. Artistic activities happen in the place that is most sensible and appropriate—usually around the dining-room table—but one-on-one activities, such as sewing, might happen in the "living-room" area. Creative play happens everywhere, as exemplified by putting a large cloth over the dining-room table for a tent, children playing in the kitchen sink as they wash up, the variety of activities taking place in the living room, and even allowing a few children to occasionally play a quiet game in the nap room when it is not in use for the purpose of sleeping. As you read further, you will discover the kind of learning that takes place with each activity.

Cleanup and Morning Snack

Soon it will be time for a healthy snack of oatmeal and apple slices. First we need to tidy up the house. Marie has taken care not to have an overabundance of toys, just the right amount to support the varying ages of children. During the day, if she notices that some play materials are no longer being used, she will go ahead and put them away or have the children do so. This avoids a lot of clutter and makes cleanup time more pleasant as well.

Marie tidies the room in the same order each day, starting with gathering all the play cloths and putting them in a large basket near the couch. Then she

starts gathering blocks, tidies the play kitchen, and puts back any furniture or chairs that have been moved to create play spaces. At some point, she quietly begins to hum and then sings a little cleanup song. She always moves around the periphery of the room and into the center, with the children helping and gathering along the way. Her predictable movement offers a level of calmness to what can often be the most chaotic part of the day. Some children get a basket and load it up to take things to their rightful places. Others tuck the baby dolls into their beds. Two children run and hide, thinking that if they lie in the middle of the room with a cloth pulled over them, no one will know they are there! After picking up a few things, I settle back on the couch to fold the play cloths and occupy two of the toddlers who were busy undoing what had just been tidied. We don't want to rush, so it takes about fifteen or twenty minutes to get everything tucked back into place.

Marie sets the bowls, cups, and spoons on the table next to the oatmeal

and apples and gets out the face-wiping cloths for after snack. The cloths are soaked in warm lavender water. At 9:15 Stefan comes inside with the two boys, and after washing up, we all come to our assigned places at the table and have a few delightful hand gesture games before eating. "Where Is Thumbkin?" is just right for the younger ones, and something a little more complicated is good for the older children:

> *Here's my lady's knives and forks*
> *Here's my lady's table*
> *Here's my lady's looking glass*
> *And here's the baby's cradle.*

Something about the warm oatmeal settles the children into a quiet mood. It also helps that the two oldest children have already been engaged in hardy work and are not compelled toward silliness right now. They really take their cues from Stefan, who, after a couple of deep breaths, dives into his oatmeal with relish, while demonstrating good manners!

When we finish snack, the children wipe their faces and rinse and stack their bowls, which Samuel loads into the dishwasher while other children wash the table. Those who need to go to the bathroom do so. Stefan starts helping children set the table for lunch, while other children start getting themselves ready to go outside. Two children busily put out placemats, napkins, and tableware. Each child has a specific place to sit, and this is identified by their individual napkin rings. The special candle, the crown jewel of the table, is the last to go on. Marie gets out the basin for warm, lavender water and clean face cloths for after lunch. The pot of soup is cooking, and I anticipate how good it will smell when we come back in.

Notes of Interest

Why does Marie tidy up the exact same way every day?

Young children thrive in predictability and consistency. The less they need to wonder what is coming next, the more relaxed they can be. They tend to get less agitated. It is ideal if they can simply dream along with

the rhythms and routines that have been established by the adults. A well-scheduled day or week has both routines and rhythms. Something like cleanup or setting the table is a routine, basically done in the exact same order each time. Routines consider the "things" that need to happen. Rhythms take into consideration the mood and how one thing flows into another. Rhythm is more like breathing, and the more the daily rhythm can have a quality of inhaling/focusing followed by exhaling/relaxing, the better.

Why is the lunch table set right after the morning snack?

It makes sense because the children are already there at the table, and then there is less to do when they come in for lunch, already hungry and

a little tired. This way, as soon as they come in and wash up from being outside, they are more or less ready to sit down and eat.

Why is lavender water used for the hand washing?

Lavender is a natural antiseptic.

Going Outside

We start getting Sasha and one other toddler ready to go out when Courtney, the four-year-old, shows up ready to help. "Hmm?" I query, and Courtney looks down to see that her rain boots are on the opposite feet from where they belong! A quick reversal and then she is ready to help Sasha with her boots. Stefan goes out with the first wave of ready children. Soon, I go outside with children in tow, while Marie bundles the baby snuggly into the buggy and follows. It is like an old-fashioned baby buggy where the baby faces the caregiver. The baby has had a morning nap and will nap again with the other children after lunch. He is so happy to be outside, and Marie parks his buggy right under a gently swaying tree—a natural hanging mobile! On colder days, there may be a woolen blanket over the buggy or he may be snuggled against Marie's chest in a baby wrap. On warmer days, a blanket is put on the ground, surrounded by straw bales to create a protected space and a natural playpen.

"Hey, Marie!" Samuel calls. "Look what I planted!" Marie sees that he has helped to plant a whole row of beans and a small flowerbed. Then he scampers off to climb the low-branched tree in the backyard. One of the two-year-olds wants to climb the tree also but is not quite capable. No one helps her. She cries for a minute, gets a gentle hug, and then toddles off to play. One of the cardinal rules is not to put a child into a position that she cannot get into herself. Better to let her struggle and strive until that special day when she can reach the first limb and pull herself up. David Elkind once used the term *markers* to indicate those moments when a child reaches a new accomplishment or receives something that he or she has anticipated for a long time. Immediate gratification eventually dampens, rather than deepens, joy in life.

Marie feeds the chickens and lets two of the children help her collect a few eggs. Then she lets the two rabbits out to roam while the children play.

Stefan decides to take the older children on a walk to the nearby woods while Marie stays behind with the youngest children. Sometimes they go into the woods also, but today it is a special opportunity for the older ones to explore more difficult terrain. I join Stefan.

"Hey, I just finished reading *Last Child in the Woods,* by Richard Louv," Stefan tells me. "It's all about the importance of playing outside. One of the studies indicates that the more wild the green space is, the more benefit the children derive. Here's what's amazing to me—significant improvements were noted in children with autism, ADD, and ADHD."

"It doesn't surprise me," I say, "when I think of how much calmer I feel when I am out in nature."

Stefan is keenly aware of the whereabouts of each child, but he has the wisdom not to hover. He sits on a fallen tree and begins whittling a piece of wood. He can put it away quickly in his backpack if he needs to rescue or intercede. From having come here many times, the children know their boundaries—how far they can wander and how high they can climb. Even Samuel is content to honor the boundaries now that he knows he will be allowed to explore. Months earlier he had pushed the limits, which resulted in being taken back to the house and told that he could only go into the woods when he could honor the boundaries.

While Samuel is young enough that they have had to set boundaries for his safety, we all secretly hope that, as he becomes older, he will be allowed to explore more and more. Children learn so much from those times when they are in a tight spot and, through their own initiative, find their way out. We love the stories of Huckleberry Finn and Tom Sawyer, yet we shudder at the thought of our own children exploring! Children who do not have the opportunity to push their physical boundaries a bit can grow into teens and young adults who lack confidence, or who have trouble discerning whether or not a risk is life-threatening. Stefan puts away his whittling to tend to Courtney, who has fallen and scraped her arm. He cleans it and puts some healing cream on it with a Band-Aid. I give a special grandma kiss and hold her on my lap for a few minutes until she is ready to venture back out. Ste-

fan gets cups and water out of his backpack so all the children can have a drink before we start back.

While we were gone, Marie and the younger children were having their own adventures back at the house. They spent a good deal of time climbing up and sliding down the sand hill. The younger of the two toddlers asked to swing in the swing hanging from the tree and would have happily stayed there the whole time. However, Marie valued the importance of self-directed movement and took her out of the swing after ten minutes. The toddler fussed for a while and then moved on to the next thing. The baby was content watching the gentle movement of the leaves and branches of the tree for a long time and then wanted some close time with Marie. She held him for awhile, then put him down on the blanket to practice rolling over.

When the little ones hear their older friends coming back from the woods, they run to the fence to greet them. Marie puts the baby back into the pram and slips back inside to change a toddler's diaper, while Stefan gives everyone else a good brushing off before they take off their shoes to go back inside. Each child places his or her shoes on a mat inside the door and puts on nonslip socks or soft-soled shoes before going to the bathroom to wash up for lunch.

Notes of Interest

Why did Marie use a stroller or buggy in which the baby faces the caregiver?

A recent London study indicates that babies in backward-facing strollers are typically less stressed because they can see their parents or caregivers. This is something Marie had noticed for a long time.

What do you do if your child care home or center does not have nature close by?

If your child care setting is not one that is blessed with a welcoming outdoor environment, do what you can to find it. Usually there is a nearby park. Even a vacant lot with a scrubby bush, grass growing up through

the cracks, and loose gravel can invoke creative play in a young child. In the book *The Geography of Childhood*, by Nabhan and Trimble, these issues are addressed.

Time for Lunch

The "washing hands song" resonates throughout the bathroom and hallway:

> *Wash hands, wash*
> *It's time to wash our hands*
> *Now it's time to wash our hands*
> *Wash our hands now*

On some days the children are given a warm footbath before lunch, but not today. Later, Marie reflected that one of the children who was having a more restless day would probably have benefited from the footbath. She and

Stefan agree to be more aware that even when they do not do something for the whole group, they still can do it for a specific child in need.

Stefan helps the youngest children with hand washing, while the older children wash their own hands, put on their dinner shirts (apron smocks), and help to put the food on the table and pour the water. Marie is warming the baby's bottle and helping the children settle at their chairs. On some days the baby's mother is able to come over and nurse her baby quietly in the other room, but today Marie will be feeding him on her lap during the meal.

Just as I had imagined, the whole house smells of the delicious soup. What I had not known is that we would also be served fresh bread the children had made the day before. There is a plate of carrot sticks and a plate of fresh pear slices to complete the menu.

Now, hands are washed, and we are ready for lunch. With all seated, a nice deep belly breath and then a song prepares and settles the children:

> *Hands together, hands apart*
> *Hands together, we're ready to start.*

With hands folded, as if in prayer, all is quiet except for the sound of Stefan striking a match and lighting a candle in the middle of the table. We sing the mealtime blessing:

> *Earth who gives to us this food*
> *Sun who makes it ripe and good*
> *Sun above and earth below*
> *To you our loving thanks we show.*

Two of the children belt it out with loud and silly voices, and Marie quietly says she is sure that we can sing in such a way that the fire fairies dancing on the tip of the candle will not be offended by our boisterousness! We sing again, this time with respect.

It is just a little after twelve o'clock. The food has been blessed, and we all take a drink of water—sometimes it is herbal tea. Stefan begins passing out bowls of soup while Marie feeds the baby. The children pass the plates of carrots and pears around the table. One of the children pours the milk into each child's cup from a small pitcher.

"Stop, Courtney!" cries Samuel. "You're gonna flow over!" Just in time I help Courtney stop pouring before the milk runs over the edge of the cup. She is still learning. They are only supposed to fill the cups one-quarter full and can have seconds when they want more. Sometimes they go several days in a row without a spill or accident. Other days—well, it comes with the territory!

At first we eat in silence, giving body and soul a chance to feel the nourishment from the warm food. Eventually quiet conversation starts—something a child saw on the walk or something happening at home. I tell a story about the family of cardinals I had seen recently at my bird feeder, and soon almost every child has a similar story to tell. Their innate drive to imitate even shows up in their storytelling. It is not lying, as some people may think. Usually very young children do not lie. They simply identify deeply with what they are seeing and hearing and then say that the same thing happened to them.

Marie tells Stefan about the visit yesterday with Mr. Taylor, their licensing

specialist. "He's still trying to figure us out," she says. "We're just so different from what he is accustomed to seeing. But yesterday he told me that he wished there were more places like ours! He was very taken with how we work with relationship-based care and how capable the children are." Not wanting to go into too much detail in front of the children, Marie finished by saying, "He also specifically mentioned how impressed he was with you." Stefan smiles.

"Hey, who was that guy that came here tomorrow?" one of the children queries. "Is he moving here?"

"That was our friend, Mr. Taylor, who came yesterday," says Marie. "He just stops by now and then to see how we are doing. He already has a house he lives in."

"Oh."

Some children ask for a second bowl of soup, and so do I! Stefan also slices a few more pieces of bread and passes them around.

About halfway through the meal, the two older boys start giggling and talking about poop and pee. Why does this so often happen at the dinner table? Could it be that as their digestion is being awakened, children suddenly remember these miracles of bodily processes that take place every day of their lives? "Let's go into the bathroom to talk about that," I suggest. Not wanting to leave the table, they decide to drop the subject and go back to eating.

"God lives on the moon," one of the other children offers.

"Nu-uh," replies another, "God lives in the sky."

Samuel shakes his head in disbelief at how misguided are these friends of his! "Listen," he says, "I know this is true. God lives in your heart!"

One of the two-year-olds gets a big grin on her face and gives Samuel a kiss on the cheek, which he accepts and then shrugs his shoulders.

Near the end of lunchtime, Charelle arrives. She will be taking Stefan's place in the afternoon, and they overlap for lunch cleanup and nap time. They give each other a quick collegial hug. She is thrilled to have found a place like this where childhood is respected and the caregivers love their work. Charelle puts on her apron, which her grandmother made for her. She loves it because it has big pockets that come in very handy, and she also likes it because it was made from a soft cotton fabric that the children can snuggle into. She usually wears it all afternoon because she is not supposed to wear jeans

or tight-fitting pants to work; and if she forgets, her apron covers her and offers a nice flowing form!

When most of the children are finished, Stefan hands out warm face cloths for them to wash their faces and hands. Then he hands the candle snuffer to one of the older children to snuff the candle. It is a rite of passage that the younger ones can anticipate coming to them someday.

"Thank you for our meal," we all sing together, and then the candle is snuffed.

Two children stay at the table to finish their last bites, while the others take their dishes over to the sink to rinse and load into the dishwasher after they scrape their leftovers into the compost bin. Then they each take a crumb catcher to their place at the table to sweep up any crumbs they left on the table or floor. I get out the big broom and sweep around them. Face cloths and napkins are put in the basin and dinner shirts returned to their hooks unless they are very soiled.

I can see the results of the focused attention the caregivers have given to these children as they learned all the activities involved with caring for their home away from home. From sorting and folding laundry, to counting out napkins and plates, to helping to prepare the food, to washing up, to learning songs, stories, and games, to experiencing the tender loving care of adults, I knew without a doubt that this is how young children are meant to learn about life.

Notes of Interest

How were they allowed to have a candle at the table, and why would they want to have one?

The licensing specialist had initially objected to having a candle on the table, but eventually he had accepted their request for an *exception,* as Marie explained how the candle provided a learning experience for the children in how to respect fire and practice safety with it. Their compromise was to only use candles that were enclosed, and they had found a beautiful globe candlestick holder. This allowed the children to still see

the beauty and magic of the dancing flame, and it created a mood of reverence for the beginning of the meal.

Why footbaths?

Warming, gentle massage, and oiling of the feet can really help to ground children if they are a bit wild or unsettled. It is a good idea to then put a pair of warm socks on them to retain the gentling that the footbath has just provided.

Time for Rest

After a warm hug from Stefan and a few hugs from some of the children, I say good-bye and go into the other room to tell Marie I will see her again next week.

Marie had slipped away to change diapers for the baby and one of the toddlers. She swaddled the baby and laid him in his bed. Then she put soft sleeping pants on the toddler, who had been wearing pants that were slightly snug around the waist.

Charelle brings the children who have finished washing up from lunch to use the toilet, wash their hands, and brush their teeth. I love the toothbrushing song that guides them through each step of brushing and lasts the right length of time for them to do a good job!

> *Brush, brush, brush*
> *Up and down*
> *Brush, brush, brush*
> *All around.*
> *Brush your teeth and brush your gums*
> *Brush your teeth and brush your tongue…*

Soon Stefan brings the last two children to Charelle and goes into the bedroom to oversee the beginning of nap time. Marie slips out for a break.

The children lie down on their individual cots. Stefan had set these up before he had gone outside with Samuel that morning. Each child had a sleeping sack made from a soft comfy blanket that had been cut to the right size, folded over at the bottom, and sewn up on the sides. The caregivers had sewn these on sewing machines one Saturday morning with a group of the parents. They were roomy enough for comfort, but snug enough to help the child feel appropriately contained and ready for rest. Underneath each blanket a lambskin lay on the cot, serving as a soft mattress. On really cold days, a hot water bottle was placed inside each of the sleeping sacks to make them toasty warm

for the children. The warmers were taken out and put away once the children went to bed. In the summer months their sleep sacks were made of lighter fabric. The children's cots were made to feel like canopied beds by placing a three-sided frame around the head of each cot and draping it with soft fabric that filters the light in the room.

Each child has a special sleeping dolly softly tucked into the sleep sack. Most of these were ones that Marie had made for them. Some of them took them home to sleep with them at night and bring back the next day. Two of the children, however, had special things from when they were babies that they cuddled with when they slept. One was a piece of a blanket that had been cuddled so much that all that was left was a few squares. The other was a little toy kitten that had been given to the child by a beloved grandparent.

Stefan draws the shades to set a quieter mood, a soft lamp is turned on, and a window is opened slightly for fresh air. Once everyone is on his or her cot, Stefan moves quietly from one child to another giving a soft back rub. Some prefer to have their forehead gently stroked. He typically does not linger but spends only a few moments with each of them, giving them the opportunity to settle themselves into rest. One child is a bit restless today and keeps wiggling her legs and arms. Stefan gently, but firmly, holds her still until she begins to relax. This technique is lovingly used to support a child with sensory challenges or who is simply a wiggle worm.

Charelle tells a story. Today the baby starts fussing, so she holds and rocks the baby while telling the story. After the story, she sings and hums a lullaby. Then she puts the baby in bed, turns off the lamp, and plays the kinderharp while the children drift off to sleep.

Stefan leaves every day at 1:30. Tonight he has a date with someone very special, and he is eager to make dinner reservations and buy movie tickets. Charelle is excited for him, and gives him a wink as he slips out of the room. She relaxes to the sounds of the children sleeping and takes a few minutes to gaze at each one of them, holding them in her heart and picturing each of them in one of their golden moments. She also ponders the loving interest of each child's guardian angel and gives thanks.

Around 2:00, Charelle leaves the nap room. She finishes up the fine-tune cleaning of the kitchen and dining area and puts in a load of laundry. Then she

prepares a simple snack of yogurt and fruit for the afternoon. She starts checking the chests of drawers that hold the children's spare clothing and remembers that she does not need to do this anymore. The parents have agreed that they will do this every week instead.

Charelle is eager for her meeting with Marie. Normally Marie would not return before 3:00, but she agreed to meet with Charelle today at 2:30.

On her break, Marie had driven to the nearest park, put on her favorite walking shoes, and gone for a walk by the creek. She had brought her current favorite book and read the next chapter. It was hard to put down, but she had one more thing she wanted to do before going back home. She stopped by the store and purchased the ingredients she needed to bake her husband's birthday cake the next day with the children. Then she called to check in with her daughter, who had play rehearsal after school.

Charelle fixes a pot of tea, and when Marie comes home Charelle fills her in on how the children settled into nap. Marie tells Charelle about the events of the morning, highlighting those things she feels Charelle needs to know about the children. They each wonder about Courtney, who tends to be a bit clumsy in her movements and mildly inarticulate in her speech. Marie suggests that they watch her movements closely over the next several days and then practice moving like her themselves to see if that will give them any fresh insights. She had learned about this from an early childhood colleague with a background in therapeutic movement. They agree to meet again next week to share what they have discovered.

Marie can tell that Charelle has something else she is eager to share and settles into the couch to listen while she sips her tea. Charelle has a twinkle in her eye as she speaks.

"You won't believe what happened in class today!" Charelle is getting her degree in early childhood education at the local university. "My professor started talking about the necessity of teaching four-year-olds the fundamentals of reading and writing, and I actually raised my hand and asked her why she felt that was important. I was so nervous! I've never done anything like that before!

"The professor then cited various regulations that were being put into place by the Department of Education and had spoken urgently about how

important it was for the United States to be competitive in business and industry.

"So, then I spoke up again! I asked her how teaching the fundamentals of reading and writing to four-year-olds through direct instruction was going to help when it was contrary to what so many early childhood experts had noted about direct instruction—it's not the developmentally natural way children that age learn.

"I even mentioned that a number of studies show that academic 'gains' from early instruction of young children were lost by the time the children were in third or fourth grade.

"I was on a roll then, so I put in a word for the Alliance for Childhood and said that numerous writings show that self-directed play, experience-based learning, and being out in nature provide the healthiest foundations for young children to grow into creative, intelligent learners."

Charelle had surprised herself by having the courage to speak up during class. She was also pleased that she had managed to speak respectfully and without raising her voice, even though she had felt her cheeks turn red.

"So, what was the professor's reaction?" Marie wondered.

"You're not going to believe this. She thanked me! And then she encouraged the rest of the students to take the question up as a point counterpoint study. I've made an appointment to meet with her next week!"

"That's great, Charelle. Way to advocate for the children!" Marie gives her an encouraging handshake.

Notes of Interest

From what materials are the three-sided frames made for the bed canopies?

I have seen two kinds. The wooden ones are made from three hollow square frames with holes drilled into them at top and bottom in order to tie them together. These are great for the children to make play houses with and are easy to move. The solid ones from cardboard or particle board are covered in fabric, which can be taken off for washing.

What is a kinderharp?

It is a simple pentatonic stringed instrument that is helpful for quieting children and also useful in setting a mood for storytelling. The pentatonic scale is naturally soothing to young children.

Are stories only told at nap time? What about puppetry?

Stories can be told anytime. For some children, it is a therapeutic moment on the caregiver's lap. Other times, the group is gathered, perhaps before snack, for a little puppet show with lap puppets or simple tabletop puppets. Three times a week, Marie gathers the children before snack time for a few seasonal circle games and a simple lap puppet show. Altogether, it is rarely more than ten minutes. Once or twice a year, she and a group of friends present a more elaborate puppet play for her children and for children at the local library.

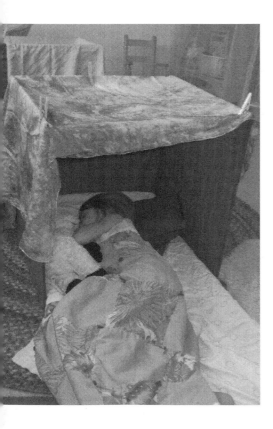

A word about advocacy

For Charelle to speak up during class took a lot of courage on her part. Many educational policies and the teaching materials they are spawning are not developmentally appropriate, nor are they in the best interest of our children. Never in the history of modern culture have we had so many children labeled with learning disorders and social/emotional disturbances. Children cannot stand up for themselves. We are their advocates, and it is time for us to stand up for them.

Why does Marie do personal things such as baking her husband's cake or making out her grocery list during her working hours?

As long as the children and the environment have been well-tended, there is no reason for a caregiver not to take care of a few personal activities that fit in well with the living arts upon which our approach to child care is founded. Baking is a domestic art, as are sewing and mending, doing laundry, and any number of other tasks. Additionally, these children know Marie's husband and will enjoy being part of the celebration of his birthday by preparing his cake. Some of them will also want to draw pictures to make him a birthday book!

End of the Day

Marie goes into the kitchen to fix the children's tea. It is getting close to three o'clock, and one of the toddlers wakes up. Charelle folds her into her arms and gives her a few moments of cuddle time. She changes her diaper and gently brushes her hair and oils her face—a refreshing start to the last part of the day! While she is doing this, two more of the children tumble in and sit on the couch, awaiting their turn for TLC. Courtney jumps up and runs to the potty, then comes back and waits. After they are all brushed and shiny, they head back into the nap room to fold up their bedding while Charelle gently awakens the remaining sleepers. With one of the toddlers wrapped around her leg, she quietly raises the window shades and begins singing:

Wake up, wake up, sleepy heads
Time to wake, get out of bed
Wake up, wake up, sleepy heads.

This used to be one of the hardest parts of the afternoon for Charelle because she was somewhat opposed to waking children from sleep, feeling they should always be allowed to wake on their own. However, she realized that if a child slept until 4:00 or 4:30, it could be doubly difficult for the parents to get the child to bed between 7:00 and 7:30, the goal they were working on with the families! It was all a work in progress, and Charelle was slowly coming to peace with her responsibility to gently awaken the children no later than 3:00 so they could have snack by 3:30—again trying not to interfere with their dinner meal with their families by snacking too late in the day.

As she continues singing the wake-up song, most of the children begin stretching and slowly getting up to go to the bathroom. The baby awakes with a big grin on his face and looks around before making signs that he wants to be picked up. Charelle changes the other toddler's diaper and then sets to work getting the last two children to wake up. Amazingly, it is Samuel who is always the hardest to awaken. He played hard when he was awake, and he slept hard when he was asleep! He resisted being awakened, but Charelle had discovered that gently wetting his hands with a warm wet cloth and then slightly stroking it across the back of his neck was helpful. Sometimes he pushed it away, but more often it gently brought him to wakefulness. He

would stare into the room for a few minutes as if he were trying to reenter the galaxy from a place far, far away! Often the first words out of his mouth were "Where's Marie?" Charelle would simply smile and say, "You will see her very soon." She picks up the baby and begins changing his diaper. She follows the same routine as Marie with the same little touching game.

Transition after nap could sometimes be chaotic, depending upon the children. Charelle had learned to trust that form returns out of chaos. Sometimes she would play a simple game with them or read a book on the couch to help them transition back into the day. On those rare days when she or Stefan substituted all day, they each developed an even deeper respect and admiration for Marie, knowing that she had done this for many years by herself.

When Marie comes into the room, she is met by cheers from the children. She helps Charelle finish the hair brushing and face oiling before they all sit down at the table for afternoon snack. Before they are finished, the father of one of the three-year-olds arrives. She runs into her daddy's arms and buries her head in his neck. Then she glances back over to Marie and Charelle with a beaming smile on her face and pronounces, "This is MY Daddy!" He helps her to rinse and stack her snack dishes and then goes into the nap space to help her put away her sleep sack and cot. Her daddy brings her back to the table for good-bye hugs from Marie and Charelle, and off they go.

In the morning, it had been the reverse ritual—hugs good-bye to mommies and daddies and warm greetings to the caregivers. Seldom, but occasionally, there were a few tears. Most of these children had been coming to Marie's for a while, and the bridges from parental home to home away from home were strong and intact.

Snack is almost finished when another parent arrives. It is clear that she has experienced a difficult day, and Marie offers her a cup of tea. She sits with her child on her lap for a while, sipping tea and breathing her child back into her. Then she and her child rinse the child's dish and put away bedding. It is nice for the parents to touch into the physical environment that their children have been in all day, even if just for a few moments. Helping with their child's dishes, checking on the nap space, and checking their child's drawer for clothes are all ways of acknowledging the home-away-from-home experience they want their child to have. In some ways it is the reverse of the home

visit. The caregiver has gone to see their family home, and now the parent expresses equal interest in his or her child's home away from home.

Charelle finishes putting away snack and checks the fridge and cupboards for staples to see if there is anything still needed for tomorrow's snacks and lunch. A menu is posted from which she can check. Marie unloads the dishwasher with Samuel and one other child. The baby is lying on a sheepskin on the floor in a protected corner of the room, cooing and exploring his toes. The lunch dishes are put away, and snack dishes are loaded into the dishwasher.

The baby's mother arrives, and the reunion is heartwarming. It is as if a vibrational field starts resonating in the room. The baby's greeting extends from the tip of his head to the bottom of his feet as he lifts his little belly and grins joyfully at his mommy, and she can hardly wait to have him back in her arms. She quickly puts new packets of breast milk in the refrigerator and then scoops him up, smothering him in kisses, and goes to sit on the couch. "Hello, my sweet baby boy," she coos to him while preparing to nurse. "I love you a bushel and a peck, a bushel and a peck and a hug around the neck." She sings him a song she learned from Marie at a parent-infant class Marie offers a few times a year. The two are left to linger as long as they want.

By 3:45, Charelle is outside with most of the children who have not been picked up, and Marie is inside sweeping and vacuuming and tidying. Two of the children wanted to stay in with her and are also sweeping. Caring for their home away from home had become part of the daily/weekly experience of these children. Rather than being given clever "curricular" materials from which to learn abstract concepts, they were learning the fundamentals of daily living, which also happened to provide them with many preacademic skills.

Charelle brings out the jump rope and ties one end to a tree. She is introducing Samuel to the joy of rope jumping. He has conquered the snake and has managed to jump over a relatively elevated still rope. Now she is starting to sway it for him to learn how to jump while the rope is moving. The two girls who were sweeping have come outside now and want to participate. Charelle does the simple snake for them, and they are satisfied.

After jumping rope, they play a few games of Mother May I. The younger children soon lose interest, but Samuel and the other older child love it. They are just learning how to really listen to instructions and follow through, while the younger ones are still primarily learning by imitation. The girls who had been sweeping with Marie were not taught to sweep by direct instruction. They simply imitate what they see every day. Samuel, on the other hand, is slowly crossing the bridge from early childhood to middle childhood, and his capacities and style of learning are subtly changing. His parents are giving him the opportunity to make these changes gently, rather than rushing him into an instructive environment full of expectations that are not necessarily in his best interest in the long run.

Marie hangs up her cleaning apron and goes outside. Charelle goes inside for one last look around, and changes out the diaper pail and garbage bins before she leaves. After she puts the garbage outside, she and Marie say good-bye, and two of the children give her a kiss before she walks out the gate. Samuel's father and another parent arrive within minutes of each other. They have a warm exchange and go inside to sign out their children and to check their extra clothing. One of the children goes in with her mother, and they sit for a few minutes having a reunion snuggle. Samuel stays outside playing; and when his father comes back out, Samuel invites him over to see his latest jump rope move.

Marie has really fostered the idea of the reunion moment when the parents pick up their children, rather than just swooping them up and going straight to the car. Those minutes of reconnection are important, and she recommends that they also have a few moments when they first arrive home—perhaps a snuggle on the couch before going into the kitchen to prepare din-

ner. Also, she recommends that parents make it possible for their child to participate with them in home activities, even if it is standing at the sink and washing something in a basin of warm water. The activity isn't as important as being near the parent for a while, perhaps even playing outside together!

The end of day is very near, and only one child is left. Marie sits in a lawn chair hemming one of her blouses. Before the last child leaves, her daughter arrives home and gives her mother a peck on the cheek. The little one runs over to her. "*Uppie*," the child pleads. Marie's daughter, who has grown up around little ones, lifts her up and gently swings her around before going inside to call one of her friends to tell her about the rehearsal. On the afternoons when she gets home earlier, she often sits outside for a while enjoying the children and vice versa. Young children love teens and preteens, and it is wonderful when there are youth who regularly participate in the lives of the children.

Marie's husband arrives just before the last parent shows up. As he gives Marie a kiss, another request for uppies comes from the little one, who this time receives a bear hug instead of a swing around. He pulls up another lawn chair to sit and drink in the atmosphere so different from his work environment. His lap is immediately filled with the child until her parent arrives. She jumps down to greet her mother and goes inside for her snuggle time and checkout. Soon they come out to say their good-byes; and as they walk through the gate, Marie takes a nice, deep belly breath. She is tired, but not exhausted, and she is grateful for her life. And that, perhaps, is the greatest gift that she gives these children every day—a life full of "Yes!"

Notes of Interest

What happens when older children do not nap?

All the children rest for a minimum of a half hour after the story is told. This is required by most child care licensing agencies, and the children need a rest in the middle of the day. At Marie's, an older child is allowed to play a quiet activity or look at a picture book if she or he does not sleep. After a while, the child may help with snack preparation or

other quiet household activities. It can also be a time for the caregiver to read a few pages in a chapter book for the older children.

These caregivers seem exceptionally content in their work. Is this typical?

In a story such as this, you are not informed of any of the caregivers' back stories, those biographical stories that give insight into the trials and tribulations in a person's life. We all have them. However, of all the qualities that the LifeWays training tries to instill in its caregivers, two of the most important are resilience and joy in living. Some people might replace the word *joy* with *contentment*, that basic capacity to take whatever life brings, assimilate it, and move forward. It is also worth noting the different life gestures of Marie, Stefan, and Charelle. While all three are very active, Marie's basic gesture is from the heart (feeling the needs of the children and the parents); Stefan's gesture is in his hands, his will (sensing the physical needs of the children); and Charelle's gesture is in her head (pondering why things are done the way they are and then doing what she believes is right). They are a wonderful balance for one another and for the children. While there are times when they have disagreements, they have processes in place for working through them and commitment to being honest and straightforward with one another.

What does Marie do to help a child transition from home to child care?

One way Marie found to ease this transition was for the parents to visit her home with their child several times before leaving the child. That way the child could begin adjusting to the new environment and begin a gentle bonding with the caregivers before being left. Marie found that a short good-bye was almost always best ("I love you, and I know you are in the best place possible. I'll see you after nap."). So she liked to provide plenty of opportunities for the families to visit before that time.

There was a recent British study about levels of the stress hormone cortisol found in the saliva of children in institutional child care. The

study found that when children first entered institutional child care, their cortisol levels skyrocketed. Over time, the children showed outward signs of adjusting, no longer crying and seemingly able to leave their parents with more ease. Yet when the cortisol levels were tested, they were found to be still elevated—not as high, but still elevated. Part of the study's final conclusion was that in order for these stress levels to decline in children in child care, the care needed to be more homelike, with consistent caregivers and smaller groups of children. This is exactly what is done at Marie's and other LifeWays care settings: consistent caregivers, smaller groups, and homelike environments. It is like an oasis of care where the children become like siblings to one another in the warm embrace of their "adopted" aunties and uncles. The parents can leave, hopefully feeling as comfortable as they would if they were leaving their child with someone in their family.

LifeWays programs are dedicated to serving organic, whole foods as much as possible. How do they work with families who have a very different approach to eating?

The only environment a caregiver can control is the environment that he or she creates for the children. The parents are responsible for what happens in their home environment. Marie occasionally offered a cooking class for interested parents, teaching a few really simple yet nutritious meals to prepare. She also encouraged them toward the "All the Way Home" concept, which meant that, even if they purchased fast food, they would take it home, put it in serving dishes, set the table with real tableware, and eat family style, just as if they had prepared the food themselves.

It seems unrealistic that the parents participate at the level represented in this story—especially at the end of the day when they are tired and eager to get home.

It is true that on some days one or another parent is in a rush and does not follow through with the established routine. However, through

ongoing dialogue with the parents, a well-developed enrollment interview process that introduces the parents to various concepts, and
friendly reminders along the way, the parents come to understand the
value of creating these bridges for their children between their home
and their home away from home. It is not about "doing the caregivers'
work for them" by putting away bedding and so forth. Rather, it is about
helping their children see that they are engaged and interested in the
place where they are living when away from their parents.

Why would Samuel's parents choose to have him stay in the Life-Ways environment rather than send him on to preschool or kindergarten?

Letting Samuel stay in the home away from home he had known since
he was a toddler had not been an easy decision for his parents, even
though they loved and completely trusted Marie and the other caregivers. They had experienced pressure from family and friends to move
him into a "real" school. "What, after all, is Samuel learning?" they were
asked. They answered that he actually knew how to listen, how to do his
share of tidying, could set the table counting out the right number of
plates and glasses, had a wealth of poetry and games that he could re-
cite and teach to others, knew all of his colors, ate relatively well, and,
perhaps most importantly, had a twinkle in his eye! Still, they felt the
pressure and wondered: Was it enough that they saw him in this joyful
state each day when they picked him up; that they could see him growing strong in body and spirit; that he was very capable, even kind, with
the younger children most of the time; that the caregivers were very
cognizant of his needs and were providing him ever greater challenges?

In the end, they decided to visit some other places when Samuel
was four. It wasn't that they saw anything that made them want to run
screaming out of the building. What Samuel's parents realized these
other settings missed was the simplicity of daily living and the practical life activities, as well as the more artistic approach to learning. They
realized that Samuel would be in early childhood for only a very short

time and, in fact, that time was growing shorter every day. Then they spoke with the parents of a teenage boy who had been at Marie's years earlier. They had made a similar decision to keep their son with Marie instead of fast-tracking him. At seventeen, he was president of his class at school, enjoyed a number of sports, was doing fine academically, and enjoyed camping, writing, and staging funny videos with his friends and was generally content. So on those occasions when Samuel complained that he wanted to leave the "baby school," his parents listened patiently and assured him that his time was coming soon to move on. "All in good time, all in good time."

How does a LifeWays center or home write up its curriculum for licensing?

Licensing requirements vary from state to state and may have different formats for how they should be written. A LifeWays consultant can help with this. It is not difficult to describe the emergent skills that are being developed. For example, foundations for arithmetic are found in things such as measuring ingredients for cooking, counting napkins and tableware to be set on the table, and sorting the laundry, which also teaches color identification. In LifeWays, however, the children learn these things by imitation, not direct instruction. This is what Dr. Rudolf Steiner recognized about the learning of young children—that they learn from life itself. He did not offer advice on curriculum to educators of children under seven. Instead, he insisted that we dedicate ourselves to living with meaning, purpose, and integrity, and that the children learn through imitation and freedom of exploration. Our work is to lay the foundation for the child to learn joy in life and purpose in living. I know of no educational goals that are more profound or beautiful:

> *Receive the child in reverence.*
> *Educate the child in love.*
> *Send the child forth in freedom.*
>
> —Dr. Rudolf Steiner

We hope you enjoyed your day at Marie's LifeWays home. On the following pages you can read the ten LifeWays principles and the basic LifeWays practices for care of young children.

Please take the time to give yourself this little quiz: Look at each listed principle and each basic practice and see where you find it represented in the story. I hope this will help bring these principles and practices to life for you. Here are the ones you will not find in the story:

- Festivals: In this story it is a typical day at Marie's. It is not a birthday, nor is it a seasonal festival day. However, you can read about celebrating festivals in Chapter 7.

- Foreign language: There was not a native speaker of another language who came to Marie's on that day.

- Preschool/kindergarten: Marie does not have a separate preschool/kindergarten program associated with her home care. In the story you just read, there were special activities offered to benefit Samuel: the more rigorous nature walk, the more sophisticated gesture games and games played at the end of the day, and the opportunity to learn through helping with more challenging tasks. There are also times, particularly during seasonal festivals, when the older children create more involved projects over several weeks and have more challenging circle games and crafts. The life-based learning provided in LifeWays child care provides what young children need. However, in our current culture, many families feel compelled to have a kindergarten or school-type experience for their children, and this is why some of our centers provide such programs. The LifeWays Child Development Center of Milwaukee has a KinderHouse preschool program and a KinderForest program, each two days a week for two-and-a-half hours in the morning. These are programs that older children in the child care suites can attend. Community children who do not attend child care can also enroll in them to have a taste of a play-based kindergarten.

Enjoy your quiz!

LifeWays Principles of Caring for Children at Home and in Child Care

1. Young children thrive in the presence of parents and other devoted caregivers who enjoy life and caring for children. They learn primarily through imitation/empathy and, therefore, need to be cared for by people with integrity and warmth who are worthy of being imitated. This is the foundation for learning and healthy development.

2. Having consistent caregivers, especially from birth to three years old and, preferably, up to primary school age, is essential for establishing a sense of trust and well-being.

3. Children need relationship with people of all ages. Infants and toddlers thrive in family-style blended-age care, while older children see nurturing modeled by the adults and experience their own place in the continuum of growing up. Children of all ages can both give and receive special blessing when in the company of elders and youth who enjoy children.

4. Each person is uniquely valuable, gifted with purpose and worthy of respect throughout all phases of his or her life's journey.

5. Human relationship and activity are the essential tools for teaching the young child all foundational skills for life. Infants and toddlers develop most healthily when allowed to have freedom of movement in a safe environment. For three- to six-year-olds, creative play, not technology or early academics, forms the best foundation for school work and for lifelong learning.

6. In infancy and early childhood, daily life experience is the "curriculum." The child's relationships to the caregivers and to the environment are the two most important aspects through which the child can experience healthy life rhythms/routines. These include the "nurturing arts" of rest and play, regular meal times, exploring nature, practical/domestic activities, social creativity, music, and simple artistic activities.

7. Young children thrive in a home or homelike environment that offers beauty, comfort and security, and connection to the living world of nature. Healthy sense development is fostered when most of their clothing and playthings are of nonsynthetic materials and their toys allow for open-ended, imaginative play.

8. Childhood is a valid and authentic time unto itself and not just a preparation for schooling. Skipping or hurrying developmental phases can undermine a child's healthy and balanced development.

9. Parents of young children need and deserve support on their parenting path—from professionals, family, and one another. They thrive in a setting where they are loved, respected, and helped to feel love and understanding for their children.

10. Caregivers also have an intrinsic purpose and need to be recognized and appropriately compensated for the value of their work. They need an environment where they can create an atmosphere of "home," build true relationship to the children, and feel autonomous and appreciated.

© 2006 LifeWays North America, Inc.

Basic Practices
in the Care of Young Children

- LifeWays practices are based upon the fundamental need for relationship-based care (bonding and continuity), neurological research, and recognition of **living arts** (domestic, nurturing, creative and social arts) as central to the advancement of children's social, emotional, and intellectual skills. These practices can be applied in parenting, in family child care homes, child care centers, preschools, and extended care programs. The physical setting is homelike rather than institutional or schoollike.

- In child care, "suites" consist of small groups of mixed-age children who stay together with the same caregivers over a several-year period, creating a more homelike atmosphere and better teacher-child ratios.

- Adult and child activities include practical life skills such as building, gardening, cleaning, cooking, washing, repairing and sewing, among others.

- Movement/play curriculum emphasizes child-initiated activities that promote healthy musculoskeletal development, providing opportunities for unstructured, spontaneous movement in a safe environment. Traditional games and finger plays provide opportunities for the children to imitate healthy movement, develop proprioception, and increase both small and large motor skills.

- The children go outside in all but the most inclement weather. This helps them become more robust and strengthens their bond with the environment in which they live. A protected area is provided for crawlers and infants.

- Child guidance is based on the LOVE approach to discipline: listening, laughter, order, objectivity, versatility, vulnerability, energy, and enthusiasm.

- Natural organic foods are provided (whenever this is possible), and the children can participate in the food preparation.

- Foundation for lifelong literacy is fostered through storytelling and puppetry; through individual lap time with a book; through poetry, verse, and music on a daily basis; through drama; and through the daily interactions of play and movement in a healthy, secure environment.

- Emphasis is on loving human interaction with warm speech, live singing, verses, and stories rather than technology. LifeWays centers and child care homes are television- and video-free environments except for use in administration and adult education.

- Festivals and celebrations honoring traditional seasonal festivals, cultural backgrounds of the families, and children's birthdays are offered.

- When possible, ongoing relationships are established with senior adults and youth who visit on a regular basis.

- Community friends who speak a native language other than English

may be invited to play simple games or sing simple songs with the children on a routine basis.

- Preschool/kindergarten programs provide a developmentally appropriate, play-based approach found in Waldorf preschools and kindergartens throughout the world.

- Extended-day programs recognize the need for children to experience the nurture of a homelike setting with opportunities for relaxation, rest, and robust play.

Specific to Infants
(in addition to the applicable points above)

- Infants are provided safe environments in which to explore and move freely—no walkers, bouncers, infant gyms, or other mechanical devices are necessary.

- The infants are carefully wrapped for sleeping to provide a healthy sense of security and warmth, and caps are encouraged to protect their sensitive heads and ears.

- Infants receive daily outside time, carefully clothed according to the elements. Fresh air also supports deep, restful sleep.

- Rocking and cuddling are encouraged to develop a healthy sense of touch and movement and to promote security, bonding, and comfort.

- Physical care (diapering, clothing, feeding) provides focused time for connecting with the caregiver and may include a special song for the baby or a simple nursery rhyme and a gentle touching game. The baby will be encouraged to participate in clothing himself—for example, pulling on his own socks when capable.

- Clear, articulate, melodic speech is expected of the caregivers who are encouraged to communicate with the infants regularly throughout the day.

© 2006 LifeWays North America, Inc.

A Word About Mixed Ages

Remember the first time you were offered a food that you found totally offensive and could never imagine tasting? Then one day you gave in, tasted it, and found that you really liked it! Or maybe it was only okay, but over time you grew to love it. For me, it was pizza. I just couldn't imagine how something with all those different things on it mixed together could be yummy. For years, according to my mother, I wanted the items on my plate to avoid touching each other if at all possible. Carrots should never mix with peas! Then my cousin and I started making our own pizzas on our sleepovers. This gave me a sense of control about what was on there, and it was always the same—tomato sauce, ground beef, and cheese. At least it was a start. It was not until college that I gave in and tried a restaurant-style pizza, and guess what—it was delicious!

Isn't it true that variety is the spice of life—and no truer than when it comes to being around people! In early childhood, mixing the ages is not just about variety, however; it is about giving children the opportunity to "grow up" family-style, looking forward to acquiring the skills and abilities of those who are a bit older and looking back to the necessary care and nurture of those a bit younger, recalling in their own body-memory that they received that same tender, loving care.

If the idea of caring for mixed ages overwhelms you or makes you cringe, maybe it's not for you. However, if you have never tried it, maybe now is the time. Remember that food you love now but used to wrinkle your nose at?!

Here are a couple of short stories from two different child care homes about mixed-age child care.

What Ursula Wald Ramos of Tucson, Arizona, Experienced Several years ago, Ursula cared for a three-year-old girl who had recently been expressing occasional aggressive behavior. She had taken to beating up the dolls and saying she was going to smash them. Occasionally, she was striking out at the other children, seemingly unprovoked. Things were changing in her family, which could have played a role in her behavior. When Ursula added an infant to her child care group, she noticed that all of the children changed in their behavior. They all

loved the baby, and she specifically noted a change in the little three-year-old girl. After the real baby joined their group, the three-year-old went immediately to the baby dolls whenever she arrived, gathered them all up, and began to wrap them and care for them just as she saw Ursula doing for the real baby.

From the Journal of Mary O'Connell in Wauwatosa, Wisconsin [Mary had a home program before she opened the Wisconsin LifeWays centers.] It's Wednesday, and in my home day care, that means it's the day with the "twos"—not by design, mind you, but the way the schedule just happened to work out, I have all two-year-olds this day. Monroe, two and a half, spends his day as the child development textbooks will tell you. He enjoys being with the other toddlers, but he engages mostly in "parallel play," looking to the caregiver for ideas and inspiration. He has trouble sharing toys, and there is a bit of intervention required by the caregiver to make sure everyone is taking turns. His speech is emerging, but he doesn't talk very much with the other twos—mostly just three- or four-word sentences to the adult. Circle time consists of the caregiver singing and Monroe and the other children mostly watching, imitating a few gestures and contributing a word here or there.

It's Friday, and Monroe is here again, but this day with a mixed group of ages, from infant to five years old. Monroe enters the house with a grin from ear to ear and approaches James, age three. "Hi, James! Want to play cars? Mary get out the cars? I be fire truck, you be dump truck, okay James?" Monroe's day continues with the exuberant chattering, true imaginative play (inspired by the older playmates), eagerly sharing toys with the baby, and fully engaging in circle time. His whole demeanor has changed! He is confident, interactive, playful, and so proud of himself.

I often think of this contrast between the two-year-old room and mixed-age family-style care and feel so sorry for the children who never get to experience this natural blending of ages, which allows them to learn from the older children and care for the younger ones. If only every caregiver could experience the joy of watching children grow in a multi-age environment!

So, is it always that sweet?
(or "True Confessions from Mixed-Age Child Care")

There must be someone out there reading this who wants to ask, "Is it al-ways as blissful as the day you described at Marie's LifeWays home?"

First, I encourage you to reread the story. Hopefully, you will see that not everything went easily. Samuel had some challenging moments. One child fell and hurt herself in the woods. Charelle needed to adjust her story-telling to accommodate holding the baby. Another child became agitated and needed a little extra attention. There was inappropriate behavior at the lunch table. One of the toddlers got fussy outside. Some of the parents needed extra care.

And the answer to your question would be "No! Even with all of those little blips, there can be days that are even more challenging." We all already know as caregivers, parents, teachers, parent educators, nannies, preschool teachers, or anyone involved with young children that days are unpredictable, and that some days are harder, some days easier. Kind of sounds like life!

One thing I hear from people who have switched to mixed ages is that it has made many things much easier and some things more challenging. The stories above give a glimpse into the "much easier" viewpoint. The younger children tend to be more satisfied and joyful when they can be around older children, and the older children tend to be softened and helped to retain their childlike innocence a bit longer when they can be around the younger ones. At the same time, they tend to take on more responsibility and may be quite will-ing to do something to help with the younger children that they had resisted helping with before.

One challenge that concerns some licensing specialists is whether hav-ing children in mixed-age care will meet each child's developmental needs. Some of these concerns are based on a limited view of what comprises devel-opmental needs. However, other concerns are legitimate and must be taken into account. For example, concern for the safety of the infant must be taken into account. Depending upon the age and developmental stage of an infant in the care setting, the baby is either in the arms of the caregiver, sleeping in his private sleep space, or in a protected environment within the larger care environment where he can freely move and explore. In a very short time, the

older children adjust to having the baby around and are typically very careful when near the baby. One could say that the older children are *tendered* by the presence of an infant.

If we imagine a day with *CooCooWahWah* (the infant), *OopsyDaisy* (the toddler), *MeMineNo* (the two-year-old), *WhyWhy* (the not-quite-three-year-old), *LookAtMe* (the four-year-old), and *You'reNotMyBoss* (the five-and-a-half-year-old), it is not difficult to understand why some people might be concerned about putting all of them together. What happens when *CooCooWahWah* wants her bottle at the same time that *OopsyDaisy* wants a pony ride on your leg and *MeMineNo* and *WhyWhy* have started fighting over a doll while *LookAtMe* is begging you to notice her latest accomplishment and *You'reNotMyBoss* refuses to do anything you tell him to do?

Hmmm? Clearly the answer must be that you feed *CooCooWahWah* while *LookAtMe* gets a chance to learn to wait instead of being immediately gratified; and *You'reNotMyBoss* gets to rise to the occasion, sensing himself to be a big boy who can settle the doll argument with *MeMineNo* and *WhyWhy* by going over and playing Ring Around the Rosie with them, which *OopsyDaisy* readily joins!

This may sound impossible to you, but it is not. Children will often rise to the occasion when they know that an infant's needs must be met. Conversely, it is essential that we be supportive of the growing needs of the other children. Sometime in the course of the day, *OopsyDaisy* needs his pony ride and some lap time, as does *MeMineNo,* who also needs some time to do some climbing and other exploring activities. *WhyWhy* needs to know that you have heard her but are not going to burden her by actually answering her every query with some abstract concept that is not really what she is looking for. Rather, you will give her time to come up with some of her own answers and will answer her other questions with the magical "Hmm, I wonder?" *LookAtMe* (like all of them) needs to see you fully engaged in meaningful physical activities such as cleaning, tidying, repairing, crafting, cooking, gardening, or general tending so that she has strong sensory impressions to imitate in her creative playtime and a chance not to be so needy. And *You'reNotMyBoss* needs your unconditional love and clear sense of the *loving wall* boundary that holds him in your expectation of his growing ability to do what

is appropriate. He also needs to know that when he has created something with great care and interest, you are not going to allow the littlest ones to destroy it. Toddlers love knocking things down, and there are times when that is totally appropriate. But when you provide mixed-age care, there are times when the older children need time and protected space to penetrate their real work!

Ultimately we each need to decide for ourselves about the type of care we want to offer. As for me, I like the whole pizza! I am not convinced that it is in the best interest of children or caregivers to be with only one age of children in early childhood—where every person in the room (other than the adults) is a *CooCooWahWah*, an *OopsyDaisy,* a *MeMineNo,* a *LookAtMe,* or a *You'reNotMyBoss*. What do you think?

The Many Faces
of LifeWays

BY MARY O'CONNELL AND FRIENDS

*The greatest challenge of the day is how to bring about a
revolution of the heart, a revolution which has to start with
each one of us.*

—Dorothy Day

MY HEART ACHED as I heard the anguish in Donna's voice on the other end of
the phone line.

> I've made a huge mistake! When I toured LifeWays last year, I felt so
> comfortable there that I wanted to enroll my as-yet-unborn baby
> right away. The loving caregivers and the relaxed demeanor of the
> children made me want to stay forever. But then I visited XYZ Acad-
> emy, and they impressed me with their curriculum and their state-of-
> the art learning tools. I worried that if I didn't provide my baby with
> this early learning opportunity, she'd be behind the other kids when
> she went to school someday. So I signed her up there even though my
> "gut" wanted her to be at LifeWays.
>
> Each day, I visit my daughter's room at day care on my lunch hour
> to nurse her. The teachers are nice enough, but I've quickly come to
> realize that they never get around to the "curriculum" the program
> promises. They are so busy tending to whichever baby is crying the
> loudest while the others are camped out in swings and bouncy seats.

The teachers don't really know my baby or the others because they are constantly being rotated through the other classrooms as group sizes change. And the turnover is so high there, my daughter has gone through quite a few caregivers already. I leave there every day wanting to cry because I realize now that no amount of fancy curricula or technology can replace a loving, consistent caregiver for my daughter.

Donna regretted ignoring her instincts and bought into a sales pitch that resulted in poor-quality care for her daughter. She's not alone. Let's face it: When it comes to modern child care, we've all been sold a bill of goods.

For centuries, the young child learned all he needed to learn within the context of relationship. In the safe haven that existed at the skirt tail of Mama or the knee of Papa, the child's world was defined, his personality formed, his brain engaged, and his curiosity piqued. For most young children, the elements that existed in a healthy family were all that was necessary to prepare the child for future learning and life. With the dawn of child care centers, this model of relationship-based care slowly came to be replaced with institutionalized care.

A primary goal of child care became economic gain, and relationships began to suffer. As Donna experienced personally, the profit-maximizing model of modern child care has led to large group sizes of same-aged children, caregivers paid barely more than fry cooks at McDonald's, and staff members who move constantly from group to group to achieve the minimum legal teacher/child ratios. All of these conditions make real relationships between children, their caregivers, and parents difficult, if not impossible, to achieve.

Of course, not every child care program exists to make a fast buck. There are high-quality centers that seek to improve the quality of care by hiring well-educated caregivers and having lower child/adult ratios. They often implement strict standards in terms of safety and academic instruction. But does this more academic model of child care meet the needs of the child? Often, it does not. Many times caregivers in these academic programs have so much paperwork to keep track of—children's portfolios, lesson plans, academic skills testing, safety checklists—they have very little quality time to spend building a relationship with the children in their care. One LifeWays caregiver who until recently worked for years in the infant room of an elite ac-

ademic child care center shared her frustration with all of the paperwork that took her away from the children. She said that between all of the safety and academic standards that she constantly had to document, she felt that she rarely had time to just cuddle an infant.

Is it possible to provide healthier child care? YES! LifeWays is a model of relationship-based care, where the relationships between child, caregiver, and parent are highly valued. Studies show that even though the world has changed greatly, the young child still learns best within the context of relationship. Consistent caring adults are a necessity for the young child to develop. These studies only confirm what parents such as Donna feel in their hearts. Yet she, like many parents, still worried from an intellectual standpoint whether her child would be prepared for school if not enrolled in the institutionalized care that's come to define early childhood education. After twelve years in both a LifeWays home and center setting, I can say wholeheartedly and honestly that children cared for within the context of healthy, long-term relationships are well prepared for school and life.

One LifeWays parent from Milwaukee, Wisconsin, agrees:

> Thanks for inviting me to write to you about our family's experience having Antonia complete the LifeWays cycle from infancy to young childhood.
>
> Firstly, I am grateful for the consistent, loving homelike environment LifeWays gave to Antonia. LifeWays caregivers were Antonia's second-mothers. She often called me "Miss Jaimmie" and her teacher "Mama." This made me know how well loved she was, and that she perceived LifeWays as a safe and happy home.
>
> As Antonia grew from the suite baby to a big girl helper, I saw her complete her first journey through stages of maturity. She gently and gradually gave up her babyish ways, replacing old behaviors with new ones. There were no startling jolts so often imposed on children going from one year of schooling to the next.
>
> At LifeWays, Antonia learned to get along with other children in a confident, positive, and constructive way. She had gone from one who received the lion's share of attention as an infant to one who gave her attention to caring for little ones around her. One who shared her toys, who cleaned up willingly, who worked out conflict,

and who gladly obeyed the rules and routines of LifeWays.

And, when the time was right, she was ready to give up the comforting routines of LifeWays and take on the exciting new challenge of five-year-old kindergarten. When Antonia entered public school kindergarten, her behavior stood out from her peers. Her teacher often remarked that Antonia was a joy to have in the classroom.

I credit the media-free environment, storytelling, and structured routines of LifeWays for giving Antonia such a good foundation for kindergarten. When she got to school, Antonia knew that listening to grown-ups was a good thing for her to do. She was good at paying attention to the natural human pace of the teacher rather than being accustomed to the faster pace of electronic media.

Antonia's academic progress has remained very good. She recently received her first formal assessment as a first grader. Her highest mark was in "working cooperatively in groups." LifeWays taught her to value her peers and teachers, and to have confidence in dealing with others. I feel these lessons will be with her for a lifetime.

Relationship-based care is happening every day in LifeWays programs across the country, helping hundreds of children grow in confidence and good health as Antonia did. It is my sincere hope that this book helps you begin to visualize this kind of child care for the children in your life.

Over the years, many wise and creative souls have taken up this work in their own homes, centers, and schools, each in her own way. For as many more of you who feel called to this work, there will be even more interpretations of it in the future. A LifeWays program can take on many shapes and forms, as long as the guiding principles and practices introduced in Chapter 1 are honored. In this chapter, we'll introduce you to the work of several of our colleagues who have taken up this work called LifeWays. It is our wish that their stories will inspire you and broaden your perspective of what is possible.

LifeWays of Wisconsin

Two LifeWays Centers in Southeastern Wisconsin Offer Mixed-Age Child Care, Preschool, and a Parent/Child Playgroup

(contributed by Mary O'Connell, Director and LifeWays Training Graduate)

When I was a young, stay-at-home mom with two little boys and one child on the way, I had my first thoughts of being a child care provider. I really loved being at home with children and felt that we had such a nice rhythm established, it would be a blessing to be able to share that with an additional child as well as supplement the family income. Finally, when our third child, a daughter, was one year old, it felt like the right time to open our hearts and home to a child. It seemed all I needed to do was to put that thought out into the universe and suddenly a family appeared at our door with their baby boy who needed full-time care.

It was with the introduction of little Jake into our household that I found myself needing to more clearly define what I was doing and what I really believed in terms of the art of raising young children. Somehow, my gut instincts were good enough for our own children, but to take on the care of other people's little ones required some serious thought! Through reading and independent study, I found my way to Waldorf Education and Rudolf Steiner's picture of the young child. This really resonated with how I was already caring for children, and I became hungry for more. I attended a few workshops in my area and ultimately ended up at the Magical Years Conference in Ann Arbor, Michigan. There, a delightful woman named Cynthia Aldinger offered a workshop about a new concept of child care she was developing called "LifeWays." I learned she was beginning a training program and a pilot center in Wisconsin, only a half an hour from my home! It was fate …and I knew I needed to get involved.

I was lucky indeed to be a part of the very first LifeWays course, and I drank it all in like a sponge. Those were busy, fruitful years, as I applied what I was learning in the training to my work with young children. More families in the Milwaukee area began approaching me to care for their children, and I

quickly had as many children as I felt I could care for, plus a growing waiting list. I knew this was a concept whose time had come. I began to spend a day each week at the pilot LifeWays center, leading a parent/child playgroup and learning how the center operated from the wise women there. Then, when my youngest child headed off to first grade, I was ready.

My colleagues and I opened the doors of LifeWays Early Childhood Center in September 2002 in the Quaker Meeting House in the diverse Riverwest neighborhood of Milwaukee. In some ways, sharing our space with the church community was a bit of a challenge, but in many ways it was a blessing. The church helped support us financially in our early years by offering us reduced rent until we got on our feet. The building is at the edge of a large forested nature preserve, something unheard of in the heart of a big city, which precipitated the birth of our KinderForest, the area's only entirely outdoor preschool program (yes, even in the Wisconsin winter!). The Riverwest neighborhood is a dynamic and colorful place, full of families who value the nurturing, homelike care we provide for children. The LifeWays center has blossomed into a community that cherishes children, supports each family, and values each staff member.

Word of LifeWays quickly spread, and we began to have a waiting list of children. It became obvious that we needed at least one more LifeWays program in Milwaukee. Two home programs soon emerged: one run by a former LifeWays staff member (you can read Ginger's story later in this chapter), and the other an affiliate program run by a former LifeWays parent. These programs quickly grew and thrived as well.

Then in 2006, LifeWays of Wisconsin opened LifeWays Child Development Center in the suburban Lake Country area. The enrollment grew much more slowly there than did our first center in Milwaukee, for a variety of reasons. News of our new center traveled much less quickly than it had in the densely populated city. A program that is all about community can be a bit of a tough sell in a suburban area where many residents have moved to create some distance between themselves and their neighbors. And the parents in an affluent neighborhood, we found, had a much more difficult time putting their trust in a program that didn't promise early academic gains. We became very accomplished at finding educational studies to support natural

foods, unstructured play, and consistent caregivers! Slowly, the program began to grow, and as with the center in Riverwest, has become a community that uniquely reflects the larger community in which it lives. While the urban LifeWays children have the forest as their home, the suburban LifeWays children spend their days in the garden, growing their own food and tapping maple trees for syrup. We have also reached out to the public grade school across the street, and each day we walk over after school to pick up the little group of kindergarten-through-first-graders who finish their day with us. They bring a great deal of pent-up energy with them after a day in school, so they delight in the chance to have a delicious snack before heading outside to play, relishing their role as "the big kids."

Each LifeWays center has become a unique and amazing community of support for children, families, and caregivers.

Marcy Andrews' Home Program

From Midwife to Mother to Child Care Provider
(contributed by Marcy Andrews, Caregiver and LifeWays Training Graduate)

In the middle of lunch I am struck by how utterly delightful my two-year-old son, Antonio, is. I wink at him secretly across the table. "Why are you taking a picture of me with your eyes?" he asks with an impish grin on his face. These moments are so fleeting that I am constantly trying to take pictures with my eyes. Knowing how precious and temporary they are is exactly what brought me to this work.

When I adopted my first son, Rafael, three and a half years ago as a single mother, it was a challenge to let go of what, to that point, had been my lifeline and passion: midwifery. My calling to be a midwife had come to me as a flash of clarity and vision. For nearly ten years I had lived and breathed pregnancy and birth. It had fed my mind and heart and soul in a way I thought nothing else could. Just as it had called me, it was now asking me to let go. The new message was my little boy looking up to the angels and saying "Ga, Ba, Da," and I could not yet understand the message. For years, I had had long talks with one of my dearest friends, who is a Waldorf kinder-

garten teacher, and I had watched her raise two exceptional girls. Theoretically, I knew the importance of consistency and rhythm in a young child's life, but Rafa was an easygoing baby who willingly rode on chicken buses across Guatemala with me, lived in an extra room in a maternity clinic in a rural Mayan village, and went to births in the middle of the night riding in a backpack without complaining.

Then I adopted Antonio, and he called out the message loud and clear! When I first held Antonio at five months, he had already suffered severe illness, had been shifted from foster family to foster family, and seemed unaccustomed to being held. He had an inconsolable, bloodcurdling scream and refused to sleep for more than an hour at a time. Rafael was twenty months and toddled around with his fingers in his ears. I was completely consumed with being a mother and overcome with an enigmatic and unconditional love unlike anything I had ever experienced. I was delirious with exhaustion and suddenly rhythm and routine were stabilizing, grounding, and completely essential.

Compared with the exhilarating life of a midwife, each day seemed somewhat the same. Time was moving like water flowing, steadily in a mountain stream. There were times when the rhythm seemed maddeningly repetitive and mundane. But then there were times when I was blessed with the consciousness that each moment the stream was carrying new water that had been collected from a million different sources. Not only that, but it was feeding life downstream with unlimited potential and creativity! The monotony was carrying with it a vastness beyond my wildest imaginings. I was being called into a meditative trance that was calling me into the present like never before. In that state, I could recognize the nuances of every cry. I could understand the jokes that my boys told each other in single syllables and could laugh with them. I could follow my exploring toddler up the stairs thirteen times without getting impatient or bored. I could lie on the ground with them and feel the beating of their hearts in rhythm with my own. Here we were building the foundation for the rest of our lives, and all this was happening while we patiently, steadily watched the days roll by like water feeding life.

I had had ideals about staying at home with my children when they were young for as long as I had dreamed about having children. Providing child care

in my home would allow me the opportunity to do that, but I deeply questioned my ability to have the patience, the discipline, the inner strength, or the creativity. My LifeWays training fed my soul and expanded my thinking enough to see how each moment and each day with the children could be approached as a spiritual practice, taken one step at a time. I did not have to be perfect. In fact, the children would learn most from me when they saw me striving.

For the past year, my life has been spent almost entirely in the quiet New Mexico canyon I call home, with my phone quiet, my car parked in the driveway for days on end, and my work coming to me down our long bumpy dirt road in the form of children eager to learn and play. I still have my moments where I question it all. But in my lucid moments, I know I am on the right path. It is not a calling that has come in a flash of vision, but rather one that has crept into my bones through day after day of consistent rhythm—a rhythm that has cultivated my patience, nurtured my creativity, expanded my discipline, and gifted me love greater than I ever could have imagined.

LifeWays Child Care Society

A Mixed-Age LifeWays Center in Vancouver, British Columbia
(contributed by Margo Running, Director and LifeWays Training Graduate)

Caring for a young child is an experience that some of us take part in as we grow up. We are all personally cared for, which greatly affects how we are in the world. We observe how others are cared for, and we learn from this as well. Some of us grow up as a single child and only see a baby cared for when we are out in public as a baby is pushed by in a stroller. As families become smaller and social groupings are increasingly limited to same-age children, many children do not experience being with younger children until they have a child of their own. Now how can this child be cared for? What tools and memories can be activated to meet a baby's needs? I was fortunate to have a little sister added to our family when I was five years old. By the time I was twelve, there were many young children on my street, and my mother encouraged me to begin babysitting, which kept me busy most weekends. I went

to camp every summer, and this was so enjoyable that I took counselor training when I was a teen that led to my first camp counselor job.

Some years passed while I spent time exploring alternative healing, inner growth, and spiritual paths. After the birth of my first child, I rediscovered my interest in children and enrolled in early childhood education courses. The courses seemed to leave out basic subjects, such as how we "meet" the child, and felt too structured, so I didn't continue them. For my second child I needed child care and found a Waldorf mixed-age preschool in my town. The environment was so inviting that I enrolled my daughter and volunteered two days a week to learn more. I began taking courses at Rudolf Steiner College in Fair Oaks, California, with the goal of becoming a better parent, and this led me to their teacher-training program. By the time I graduated, I had joined other parents, and we opened a Waldorf-inspired charter grade school in Arizona. The school needed a kindergarten teacher, so I left my job as a massage therapist to take a lower salary as the teacher. It felt right in my heart.

Before long, I realized I was drawn to working with younger children. Looking around my community, I found a duplex home, purchased it, and opened a child care program for ten children. I developed the program based on my studies at Rudolf Steiner College and my experience with young children. After a year in business, learning from scratch how to do bookkeeping, payroll, advertising, and so forth, I heard about the LifeWays training. My experience at Rudolf Steiner College had been so good; I was excited to deepen my understanding of the young child with another training.

The LifeWays training coursework was so rich and inspiring; it was similar to my earlier training, except the focus was much more on the first three years of life and on working with mixed ages. Both trainings spoke of the inner work of the adult, but LifeWays added to that the practical and nurturing elements of working with the young child. Most Waldorf early childhood trainings focus on the social and creative aspects, how to observe the child, and what to bring the children in daily activities. I feel the gift the LifeWays training brings to the Waldorf early childhood community is the attention given to the homelike activities that are so important for rhythmical and developmental growth of the child, as well as the nurturing arts that are vital to a child's sense of well-being. Adding to my appreciation of the Wisconsin

training was that I had never before been to the Midwest, so I had never seen a red barn or a firefly!

So much of what was offered in the LifeWays course I was already doing in my home child care business. This affirmed to me that this is what it looks like if one takes an anthroposophical understanding of the young child. The areas in which I needed a lot of help were in the business realm: developing a business plan, attracting families, and upgrading the environment beyond just a home where children play.

As my daughter neared high-school age, I wished for her to continue with the Waldorf curriculum. So I put out my resume all over North America to Waldorf schools that had an early childhood department (for me) and a high school (for her). The Vancouver Waldorf School in British Columbia, Canada, gave me the best job offer, as they were just building a new early childhood center that had space for the first child care center in the world within a Waldorf school. I arrived there in 2004 to help them set up the program. We had twelve children under three years and four staff members. Licensing regulations were similar to those in the States, so it wasn't difficult to begin. The big difference within the school community was that we operated all day, all year, while the preschool and kindergartens in the same building had morning programs with a separate aftercare ending at 3:00 PM, and were closed for summer and many school breaks. So once a child turned three and left the child care program, working parents had to figure out how to find care for their child around the somewhat restrictive school schedule or take time off from work.

After two years, our child care program left the school and created a separate nonprofit society and moved to a new location, ten minutes from the school. We are in our third year of business with balanced financial books every year. We have two programs of eight children each, babies to three years, and ages two and a half to school age, per licensing requirements. Just this year, licensing has changed the rules to allow a mixed-age program, babies to school age in the same room: the original LifeWays model.

What are some things we have learned? Care of the young child asks us to care for ourselves. Young babies take in everything we are as we care for them. They digest this along with the food they are eating, and it all adds to the being into which they will grow. A child moves in response to inner urges as well as

outer stimulation. A calm caregiver "feeds" a child in a certain way, as does a nervous caregiver, each nourishing the child with a very different energy. The imprinting goes deep into the being of the child. Caregiving is a responsibility that cannot be taken lightly. A child imitates who we are in mood, gesture, and tone. This all gives us more reason to pay attention to what we are putting out to another. What does our voice sound like? Did I place the cup on the table with a purposeful gesture, or did I just plunk it down? How am I processing something stressful that happened yesterday? Am I mad at the world, or can I calmly see my role, act on what is needed, and let the rest unfold? Caring for the young child can be the most intensive task toward developing self-awareness, as the child will reflect back to us all that we are. It can be deep spiritual and soul work, if we choose to accept this responsibility to self and others.

Can we truly take responsibility for our effect on the world? Can we choose to make a difference? Care of the child is caring for the future. The child will take what we give and bring it into the future, going beyond where we have been. Can we make the future a better place by asking for self-awareness and accepting the possibility for change within our habits and responses? This is why I love this work. It is a dance between totally selfish reasons—I get the opportunity to become more aware of myself—and totally altruistic reasons—I have the opportunity to serve the world with kindness, attentiveness, and openness to others.

LifeWays House

A LifeWays Representative Home Program in Milwaukee Offers Nurturing Care for Children from Infancy to Five Years

(contributed by Ginger Georger, Caregiver and LifeWays Training Graduate)

In 2002, I was working in a child care center associated with a local grade school and sending my boys to a Waldorf school, and I was very disheartened by what I was seeing in my work life compared to the richness of experiences my boys were getting at school. I was longing to work somewhere that allowed children to be children. When I opened my latest issue of *Tamarack*

Talk, the Waldorf community news from my sons' school, there was my answer. A new child care center was being formed—one that worked out of Steiner's principles—called LifeWays. And they were looking for a caregiver! I called Mary O'Connell and interviewed for a primary caregiver position for this center that didn't yet exist. All summer, I waited to see if the enrollment would be sufficient for LifeWays to hire me, and by September I began with a full suite of children. I started the LifeWays training the following summer. Since that time, my boys have grown (one is off to college and the other is in high school), and I have moved on to run a little LifeWays program in my home with eight children.

I simply loved working with the women at LifeWays Early Childhood Center. Now that I am going it alone, I miss the nap time colleague meetings and the festivals we would prepare together, and the support we offered one another. When there were challenges, I would have someone to talk to almost instantly. For example, if a parent spoke to me in a harsh way or a particular child was running me ragged, I had help in the form of my colleagues. Now that I'm working alone, I've had to figure out ways to cope, maybe a monthly meeting with a colleague in the same field or a nap time phone call to a friend. Sometimes it's a cup of tea and chocolate at nap.

It's hard to run the whole show: invoices, attendance, phone calls, advertising, taxes, receipts, programming, care of the children, cooking, cleaning, house repairs, animal care, mending, festivals, potlucks, yard work, gardening, field trips, daily walks. Boy, I'm sure I'm missing things, but I think you get the point. Sometimes I am overwhelmed at the whole picture; but when I let go of time, I find it all gets done in the perfect time. Yes, it would be easier with an assistant, but I guess I do well under pressure and work well by myself.

The upside to being at home is, it's *home.* The children are in a home, not a center that tries to function like a home. There's a kitchen where lots of cooking takes place, real housework to be done, things to be repaired, and laundry to be folded and put away. Children learn to wait while I put lunch on the table or a baby needs a diaper change, and there's certainly nothing wrong with waiting. I might even hear them join in as I am singing to the baby while changing the diaper.

I love being home. I love baking and making organic food for the children. I love being outside in the gardens here at home. We have bunnies in a hutch; the children love feeding them and chasing them out in the yard. Then there's Zeus, our dog, whom the children simply love. This past summer the children helped to build a simple climbing frame with one of the dads, and we were able to modify it on the spot according to how the children were using it. I learn something every day. One thing I've learned is to let go of time. I've learned patience...humor. When all is crazy, we take a walk. Or sometimes we start a project to help ground everyone, even the littlest child.

One day last spring, I had a housefull plus one extra—nine all together— and it was chaotic. The children were all at one another and I was feeling overwhelmed when I suddenly got a brilliant idea to wash windows. Yep, nine children and one frazzled caregiver washing windows. No, not with Windex, but actually taking the storm windows off and washing the windows properly— a good spring cleaning! Something happened. I was busy singing and washing windows, and every child from age one to five began to play a deep, soulful play. The fighting and disconnected play that had existed before the window washing was replaced with hearty, loving play, the kind that comes out when adults are doing what adults are supposed to do...work.

Did I know the play would change? Maybe on some level that was what I desperately hoped for when I began the project; but it still surprised me, and it reminded me that I am an adult whose job it is to do useful and productive work around the children. My work enhances the children's resources and provides them with activity for proper imitation during their playtime. Thank heavens for the lessons, be they large or small!

Spindlewood

A Waldorf School Off-Site Kindergarten in Maine
Embraces LifeWays

(contributed by Susan Silverio, Director and LifeWays Training Graduate)

No one was more surprised than I to find myself waking up early one morning in 2004 and saying "Yes!" to LifeWays. I had cultivated the Waldorf kindergarten here on the grounds of our home, where Ashwood Waldorf

School first took root in 1986. As the school grew up and expanded onto a more central campus, this kindergarten continued as an off-site mixed-age kindergarten, becoming a "branch" of Ashwood. With the help of many parents, the tiny cabin was enlarged three times; and when it was complete, we named it Spindlewood. I held on to the ideal of the Waldorf kindergarten, reclaiming the traditional "children's garden" from the conventional modern academic model of pre-first grade.

Meanwhile, on the main campus of Ashwood Waldorf School, the mixed-age kindergarten had proliferated into a patchwork of programs for early childhood, specialized by age, with an aftercare program attached with additional staff. Although as a Waldorf school we still feel passionate about the same teacher carrying a class through grades one through eight, our youngest children went from teacher to teacher and classroom to classroom. The school was noticing that a nursery program with a small number of children, and a separate afternoon staff for them, was not financially feasible. For my part, I began to question how we could provide young children with more continuity of caregivers with whom they could bond and a more familiar environment where they could gain the sense of mastery and security that could free their imagination. I was also hearing a call from parents who were still attempting to keep their children central to their lives but needed a larger portion of time to focus on their work during the daylight hours.

The time was ripe for Ashwood to consult with Cynthia Aldinger, director of LifeWays North America. In the course of our conversations, while still working as part of a Waldorf school, I found myself experiencing a shift in focus to relationship-based care and an increased appreciation of ordinary life. This life included the living arts of nurturing, domestic and social arts, with the creative arts revolving around the seasonal festivals. The shift was a re-visioning of the morning program to an 8:30 AM–3:00 PM day that allows time for the nurturing physical care of the children and includes children in the daily work and play of life. Rather than the fairly intense three-and-a-half hour program of structured activities often found in a kindergarten (framed with hours of adult-only preparation, cleanup, parent contacts, and seemingly endless faculty meetings), the door was now opened to living with and around children, weaving in stories, games, and verses throughout the day.

With this shift, there seemed to be time to breathe. I was reminded that my colleagues in remedial training have for some time recognized the need for remedial work for today's children. Although I had participated in a number of courses and seminars, there had never seemed time in the course of a kindergarten morning for some of the individual care and attention needed by children. LifeWays' inclusion of the nurturing arts introduces natural activities of hair brushing, lavender face cloths, and warm lavender footbaths that allow the possibility of close observation of the child. This bodily care also meets two of the lower senses identified by Rudolf Steiner as the sense of life and the sense of touch. The afternoons also allow a "siesta time," when the assistant teacher sets up mats framed with colored cloths, so that each child has a little house somewhat like the ones that they build for themselves during imaginative playtime. Although this custom flies in the face of our hectic "on to the next activity" culture and has been met with resistance by some children, over time, the afternoons have become a chance for a true "outbreath" from the morning, a time to exhale and be restored. Often children can be heard crooning the day's songs before falling into a sound sleep. The ones who don't sleep can rest quietly as they wait for others to sleep. A very active seven-year-old boy finds quiet, rhythmic satisfaction by finger knitting during this time. The rosy cheeks of the sleepyheads as they arise testify to their sense of life and well-being.

Even a welcome change can mean the loss of the familiar, and so it was with my LifeWays transition. Like a caterpillar in a newly formed chrysalis, I found my regular morning dissolving into a bit of chaos until new rhythms and forms could emerge and hold a wider range of daily life. I felt challenged as I stepped out from my teacher role and closer to the parental realm. I even missed the familiar excitement of the often painfully interminable faculty meetings.

But what has been gained? The slightly more relaxed rhythms have allowed the assistant teacher to emerge as a person in her own right, and she has discovered a deep well within herself of stories and vignettes that amuse and delight the children, and sometimes meet them in a curative moment. We rejoice to see the children who were quiet and withdrawn last year now becoming more playful.

I sense a new feeling of quality with the parents. If perhaps I have been a

warm teacher, I now stand as a caring person in the lives of their children. Parents seem a bit more relaxed as well, and I now notice them holding, nurturing, and playing with their children when they greet them. Because there are now two pick-up times (after lunch or after siesta), there is no longer one grand dismissal time. When parents arrive to pick up their children, there is now a bit more flow, like a tidal pool effect. At the end of the morning, one child might invite a parent in to see his puppet play. At the end of the afternoon, someone might arrive a few minutes early and offer to help us tidy up. I have at times felt defensive of our kindergarten mood but now want to cultivate an atmosphere of hospitality. Life abounds in these moments, and I find that parents are grateful and respectful.

What else is gained? In spite of my own resistance to being still for a while during siesta, I am learning to have a full twenty-minute out-breath myself after the back rubs and lullabies, a moment of meditation that provides rest for my soul, even while staying in tune with the children. During the quiet time that follows, I can weave in a few other duties that I would have done in the afternoon anyway: folding a basket of laundry, having a conversation with a parent, or setting up for the next day. Also gained are several children who could not have been accommodated in a more formal kindergarten morning. Some are young; others require a bit more adult interaction to find their way through the day. The other children, some of whom have no siblings at home, gain the opportunity to observe a younger child being cared for. The simple acts of assisting a child with dressing and undressing for outdoor play nourish the sense of touch and can be a nurturing activity if not rushed, and perhaps accompanied by a song. A child who has difficulty entering into social play in the morning becomes quiet and observant as I brush his hair before he enters the room. This nurturing touch seems to bring him into his own body and allows a smoother transition into the group.

In 2006, we began our twentieth year as a Waldorf kindergarten. Spindlewood had grown to a strong and nourishing community. The time had come to create an educational organization distinct from Ashwood, the Waldorf school I had parented. My work is still with the mixed-age three-day kindergarten, and I am also directing the LifeWays training here in the Northeast. A new chapter has begun.

The Orchard

The Story of a LifeWays Program in Madison, Wisconsin
(contributed by Jacqueline Beecher, Founder and Waldorf Educator)

My daughter Leah and I wanted to meet the child care needs of families with young children. We understood that the care of young children is a legitimate and honorable need of parents, whether it be for work or respite. We are both teachers by profession. At the time we began the program, Leah had taken a break from her career as a public school reading specialist because she preferred to stay home with her two young children. And I was an experienced Waldorf teacher who had recently relocated to live closer to my grandchildren while they were little. We were both newcomers to Madison, a nice, livable, family-oriented city with no Waldorf school at the time.

Leah and I took a weekend seminar with Cynthia Aldinger at the Milwaukee LifeWays center and made our decision to go for it. We were especially inspired by the importance of having outdoor space readily available for young children, as well as opportunities for work and play. We looked for a house that had several living quarters on a large lot within the city of Madison. We were lucky to find a house on more than an acre of land! It was heavily treed and fenced all around—an island and safe haven in the city. There was a "mother-in-law" apartment on the ground level of the bi-level house complete with a kitchenette and bathroom. A large open studio and a laundry room completed the ground level, so it had enough space—the right kind of space—and we only had to paint and get furniture. The ground level would be perfect for the child care program while my husband and I could make our home in the upper level.

The house had been neglected, so we had many months of major improvements to the outside of the house before we could seek licensing. We were able to sell our former house and keep enough of the equity to make the improvements. We are happy that the house has three fireplaces, because wood carrying and wood splitting have been an important aspect of the work that children are able to participate in. We have chickens (four are permitted in the city), a large garden, fruit trees, and berry bushes; and we keep

a path open through the little woods. All of these have become important as outdoor work opportunities for the children, as well. My husband put down a cement path for trikes, and he designed and built a large sandbox as well as a water pump the children can use.

Leah and I developed a nurturing space inside. I borrowed money to equip the space with furniture, suitable play things, and so on. We met to plan a rhythmic program, then we created a policy book, applied for licensing, and began to advertise using simple flyers that we posted around. We also used craigslist.com to advertise.

We began in the fall by offering a full-day program (7:30 AM–4:30 PM) with an option for half days. Our morning program has a different activity each day: baking bread, making soup, painting, handwork, and cleaning. We charge an annual fee paid over 10 months. Our summer programming is not child care per se, but rather we offer week-long art camps for children aged either four to six or six to nine years.

When we began, we wanted to be flexible, so we accepted as few as two mornings as a minimum enrollment. We began that first year with three children who came two mornings per week. We just went with it, even though we had two adult caregivers for three children. We actually came to appreciate how those first few months of only a few children helped us to work through the kinks in our space and in our program. We began to pick up more children in the late fall of our first year. One family found us because I was a member of the Waldorf Early Childhood Association (WECAN) and was listed on their site. Another family found Cynthia Aldinger's contact information, and she sent them to us. Since that first year, all of our enrollments have come via word of mouth. By June of that first school year, we had five children and were running four mornings per week.

Our enrollment has continued to build over the years since 2003, first to five mornings and then to include afternoons. We are now completely filled, licensed for eight children as a family child care, and have four to seven children staying every afternoon. Leah has since moved to Colorado, but several excellent caregivers have come to be involved in the program, including my other daughter, Jessica.

Since The Orchard opened, the Madison School, which has applied for De-

veloping Status with the Association for Waldorf Schools of North America (AWSNA), has also opened. We work together, often sharing festivals (Halloween and the Advent Spiral, to name two). The three of us who work at The Orchard also work at the school in various capacities. The Madison School and The Orchard are trying to consciously support each other and not be in competition, and both entities are growing in spite of some duplication of programming. The Orchard serves children ages nine months to nine years, and the Madison School has a two-day Wonder Garden for two-and-a-half- to three-and-a-half-year-olds, as well as the traditional Waldorf kindergartens for three-and-a-half- to six-year-olds.

Rainbow Bridge LifeWays Program

A Mixed-Age Large Child Care Home in Boulder, Colorado

*(contributed by Faith Baldwin, Director, Caregiver,
and LifeWays Training Graduate)*

I did the LifeWays training in 2005 while working at Boulder Waldorf Kindergarten as an assistant in the toddler classroom, then as the lead teacher for two years after I completed my training. I loved my time there, but I was frustrated not having a real mixed-age program, as licensing regulations for child care centers in Colorado prohibit mixed-age programs for toddlers. Also, I wanted to be able to make a real livable wage instead of just scrape by. When my mother expressed interest in helping me start my own LifeWays program, I jumped at the chance. We opened Rainbow Bridge in August 2008 after first taking some practical steps.

The first step was to figure out what our program would look like and where it would be. After looking at licensing options, we decided that a Large Home Daycare license would be the best option for us, allowing us to have up to twelve children per day, ages one to five. We started looking for a house to rent that I (as the licensee) could live in and encountered one of our first challenges—most prospective landlords were not open to renting to a home child care. Eventually we found a house that met all of our requirements, with a fully fenced backyard and both a living room and a family room.

I moved into the house two-and-a-half months before our program opened, using this time to prepare the space both indoors and out, get licensed, and work on enrollment. We made brochures and did mailings, flyered the neighborhood, introduced ourselves to all of the area Waldorf schools, and advertised in local parenting publications.

We opened our doors in mid-August with eight to nine children per day enrolled. However, we didn't have everyone start at once. We started out with four or five children per day and added children gradually over the first month until everyone was there. This ensured that all children got as much "hip time" or "lap time" as they needed, and we had a wonderfully tear-free beginning. Also, this gave us time to work out the kinks of a new space and working together as a team.

Today my program is halfway through its second year, and it is thriving. I have visions of moving it to a center eventually and having room for classes and workshops for parents as well. I love working with the LifeWays model, and would love to see LifeWays programs available for families in every town in America.

Other Facets of LifeWays

BY CYNTHIA ALDINGER AND MARY O'CONNELL

Strengthen a parent…and you strengthen a child.

—Fred Rogers

Play is the highest phase of child development—of human development at this state.… It gives therefore joy, freedom, contentment, inner and outer rest, peace with the world. It holds the sources of all that is good.

—Friedrich Froebel

What Is a LifeWays Parent-Child Playgroup?

BY CYNTHIA ALDINGER

From the time the LifeWays project started, it was our intention to be there for all parents, not only for those who needed child care support. Some parents who wanted to be home with their children still wanted community with other parents, but often there were not many families at home in their neighborhoods. Other parents wanted a place where their children could play with other children in a protected environment. So we started a parent-child program one morning a week for two-and-a-half hours in ten-week sessions.

Our goal was not so much to entertain as it was to "be" with these families in the framework of the living arts. We knew that we wanted to be both inspiring and practical and to support families by encouraging them to find the profound in simplicity.

So, while we offered handouts and one or two evening meetings without the children to discuss parenting questions and other pertinent topics, we primarily wanted the parents to have a relaxed, good time and perhaps pick up a few new skills.

Over the years, I have experienced different parent-child program styles and have experimented with my own. I have included a schedule I particularly enjoyed with a parent-child program I did in my own home many years ago. I drew my inspiration from Mary O'Connell's laid-back style in her parent-child programs at the Wisconsin LifeWays centers.

Always a lover of mixed ages, my parent-child program was open to parents with children from infants to five- or six-year-olds. Occasionally even a slightly older child would come along. We came to be more like an extended

family getting together than a formal program. However, we always had the same rhythm and basic routines so that children (and the parents) could relax in knowing what was coming next.

As you can read on our parent-child handout, limiting the age is recommended in the parent-infant program. This program focuses on helping parents learn how to observe the developmental stages of their babies and perhaps learn some lovely, nurturing activities, some lullabies, and some simple interactive baby games. If you are interested in locating a parent-infant program near you, try contacting the Waldorf Early Childhood Association of North America (www.waldorfearlychildhood.org).

The document on the following pages describes suggested practices for parent-child groups.

Cynthia's Mixed-Age Parent-Child Playgroup

When our pilot LifeWays center was only one-and-a-half years old, my husband's work moved us out of Wisconsin back to my childhood home, Norman, Oklahoma. I thought my heart was literally going to break having to leave this new project so early in its development. Yet you can imagine my delight when a group of young parents in Norman asked me to offer a parent-child playgroup for them. It felt a little like climbing back into the saddle again.

We began with a gathering of the parents on January 6, Three Kings Day. We shared a special festival cake with treasures inside and talked about their wishes for the program we would offer.

It was a wonderful learning curve for me to offer this program in my home. Like Ginger's discovery of how nice it was to offer child care in her actual home, I, too, discovered the delight of not needing to set up a *homelike* environment for these families because we were already in a home. There was no need for play equipment for the children. We turned a couple of our easy chairs backward and placed a big piece of silk over them to create a little playhouse with a sheepskin rug and a few dolls inside. We used a small coffee table for the children to set up their tea parties and other imaginative play. I had a few dress-up clothes and plenty of silk scarves for them to play with. We always had a few sheets of paper and crayons should a child want to draw or color and a tiny area with a few infant toys for the youngest participants.

Suggested Practices in Parent-Child Programs

We do not expect all of these components to be in every parent-child program but offer you a variety of ideas from which to draw.

- The parent-child program provides a beautiful, nurturing, and homelike environment where families come together to explore the wonders of childhood. This supportive learning community promotes open dialogue and discussion about parenting choices.

- The program curriculum is based upon and inspired by the developmental picture of the young child as described by Rudolf Steiner, the founder of Waldorf education, and other developmental theorists that resonate with that developmental picture. Parallels are also drawn to current research on early childhood development.

- The parent-child program helps parents understand the great significance of their child's development as he moves through the major phases of play in the first years of life: play arising from the body, or sensory-motor play; play arising from imagination and imitation; and intentional pretending.

- The program provides parents with a circle of support in a nonjudgmental, welcoming community in a time when parenting often does not come easily or naturally.

- Parents and children together are nurtured through the daily and seasonal rhythms woven into the class content prepared and guided by the parent-child teacher.

- Rich resources are given to the children to support their play within the context of the parent-child activities.

- Simple games provide songs, rhymes, and movement for parents and children alike to enjoy.

- The children play with simple, natural materials and toys that protect and encourage their imaginative capacities and enrich their sensory experience.

- Within the activities of play provided in the program, children integrate the world and practice their life skills such as movement and balance, sensory

integration, speech and language capacity, social and emotional interactions, and imaginative and cognitive development.

- Story time brings the magic of speech and language through simple puppet plays telling the delightful stories of the nursery rhymes and nursery tales.

- The domestic arts such as baking and snack preparation, craft activities, gardening, and caring for the environment also provide the children with examples to imitate from the adults around them.

- Nurturing care such as hand and face washing and hair brushing or a gentle hand massage or foot rub may also be experienced.

- Parents learn through direct observation of the children, particularly in the parent-infant programs, and through discussion time with the teacher and reading materials centered on child development and issues pertaining to parenting and family life.

- Parents may also engage in a comparative study of ideas about child development and family styles throughout history and in different cultures by looking at families and children through the visual and literary arts.

- Parents explore together their educational values and questions pertaining to family life.

- Parents become resources for one another and develop a sense of community and "neighborhood."

- Seasonal festivals are celebrated, establishing a connection to the greater cosmic rhythms that sustain us. This rhythmic experience helps parents as they seek to find their own balance with their children in home life.

- Parent-infant classes and parent-toddler classes have a particular focus on child observation and may not include all of the components listed above, such as story time. Rather, the emphasis is on the direct relationship between parent and child and understanding development in the first year or two of life. Special emphasis is placed on observing the child's movement and allowing for plenty of floor time. This work is particularly inspired by the studies of Hungarian pediatrician Emmi Pikler and others who understand the need to give the young child freedom to move as a foundation for healthy development.

Content for this document was created by Christine Culbert and Peggy Alessandri, early childhood educators and friends of LifeWays.

General Schedule of Cynthia's Mixed-Age
Parent-Child Playgroup (2½ hours)

9:00 AM Arrival

- Coats in closet, shoes in entryway.

- Activities for the day written beautifully on blackboard in entry way.

- Family bread making: Families take turns at the table making their bread. Everyone made the same bread style (rolls, pizza, pretzels, or cinnamon rolls) for that particular day. The bread dough was waiting in a big bowl on the table when they arrived. When not bread making, they moved to any one of the following activities:

  - Veggies and fruits cut up—bowls, cutting boards, knives set out on tables
  - Butter to be unwrapped, cut in pieces, and put on butter plates
  - Ironing board and placemats to be ironed
  - Napkins to sort and fold
  - Some children went off to play right after bread making with their parents.

- Inevitably, some parents would venture off with their children until they felt the children were comfortably placed and ready to "separate." The rooms were set up so that there was easy flow between them.

9:30 AM Cleanup from food preparations, and ironing and folding. One person in charge of keeping awareness of baking bread.

9:40 AM Crafting. Sometimes it is nice to do one craft for the entire eight-to-ten week session. We worked on one thing for a few weeks and then changed projects. Typically during craft time, the parents and I would have simple conversation around parenting questions or something they had read. I found that more in-depth conversations were better saved for a parent evening without the children.

10:05 AM Cleanup from crafting.

10:15 AM Game time. Simple interactive seasonal games and songs—the same ones every time for the whole ten-week session. The last song led us to hand washing in bathrooms [Side note: Mary O'Connell often did something in her playgroup at this time that I truly love. She would pass out the children's individual hairbrushes, and the parents would brush the children's hair before snack. The parents had individualized the hairbrushes by painting the handles during one of the crafting times.]

10:30 AM Snack
- Families help set up tables, placemats, napkins, bowls, food, candles, etc.
- One parent and child prepared the warm face cloths for after eating.
- After everyone was seated, candles were lit on each table.
- Blessing.
- We ate and communed with one another while being aware of the children.
- Candles snuffed (snuffer passed from table to table) when first family to finish was ready to leave table. This was not rushed and children learned to wait.
- Warm face cloths for the children when finished.
- When each family was finished they went together to the kitchen to wash and load their dishes in the dishwasher or wash and put them in the drainer.

11:00 AM Simple puppet play. I set this up while the families were washing up.

11:10 AM Outside to the greenway behind our house with creek and trees to climb.

11:30 AM Good-bye song. Some families stayed and visited while children continued to play.

There were a few small treasure boxes for younger children to enjoy taking things out and putting things in. It was all very simple.

In the larger open area of the living room, we set up a few card tables for food preparation, and we sat on the couch, chairs, and floor when we worked on our other projects. Our first project was to sew simple playgroup aprons for the children using kitchen towels. Simply turn down two corners, sew a seam, and run a cord through that to go over the child's head and tie behind the back. We twizzled the cords with nice wool yarn. Each family had their own handwork basket, so they could put away their work whenever they wanted. In case a child wanted to participate, we had small embroidery hoops with burlap fabric and large-eyed, smooth-tipped needles for them to sew with yarn. Some families worked on the apron for a few sessions, doing fancy embroidery on the front, and some finished theirs in one session. The children used these aprons whenever they attended playgroup. Other projects included making wet-felted play balls and sawing fallen tree limbs into bundles of wood to give to the children's fathers for Father's Day. We also had a session where the children and I made Mother's Day gifts while the parents transformed a large refrigerator box into a playhouse. The parents cut all the windows, doors, and skylights into the cardboard, framing them with colored tape; then the children painted the box.

Each session began with the preparation of the bread we would be eating for snack that day. As families arrived, they would take turns making enough rolls for their family. Also set up were tables for cutting up fruit or for unwrapping and cutting the butter to go on plates for each table at snack time. We also had the ironing board set up for ironing the placemats and a table piled with our napkins to be sorted and folded. Two particular little girls always chose to fold the napkins with their mothers and grinned with accomplishment as they carried them to the dining table.

You can read how the rest of the morning unfolded. It was such a joy and privilege to meet with these young families. We had several fathers in the group, and one family even brought along the biological dad and the stepdad. Some grandparents occasionally joined as well. There is no specific template for how to do a parent-child program, but I highly recommend this family-style approach.

What Is LifeWays Forest Kindergarten?

BY MARY O'CONNELL

The natural environment surrounding a LifeWays program often inspires a new idea, a fresh way of inviting children to interact with the natural world. Just as Marcy's inspiration to start a CSA with her children led to KinderFarm (introduced in "Creating Your Community of Care"), so the impulse for Life-Ways Milwaukee's children to immerse themselves in the life of the forest led to KinderForest.

In KinderForest, every tree is a jungle gym; every fallen log a balance beam; every leaf, flower, snowflake, stick, and shell a gift from nature. KinderForest children get to live in the forest along the river behind the LifeWays center two mornings per week. This natural world becomes our "home away from home" from 9–11:30 AM these two mornings, from Labor Day to Memorial Day.

Here we discover the river's and forest's changes since our last visit. We take long hikes, climb trees, and look for tracks and treasures in all sorts of weather. In the winter we slide on ice, make snowmen, and explore the frozen wonderland Jack Frost and King Winter have created.

Each day we celebrate being in nature with songs, poems, and circle games. We share a snack together, upon a picnic blanket in spring and fall and sitting upon logs or icebergs in the winter. We may work on a nature craft or other project. We enjoy a nature story, fairy tale, or simple puppet play.

If the weather is too inclement, we come inside early and continue to share a Forest Kindergarten experience together until it's time to say "Bye, bye, butterfly."

For families who value fresh air and physical activity, nature exploration and appreciation of its beauty, and getting their hands and jeans dirty, the Forest Kindergarten program is just the thing.

What Is LifeWays Preschool?

BY MARY O'CONNELL

Having programs that pull the older children out of the mixed-age suite is not a necessity. Life is so rich in the suite, it becomes clear that the preschool-to-kindergarten-age child can have all the experiences she needs right within the "suite family." Parents, however, are often looking for an enrichment experience for their child who will be heading to school soon. It's also lovely for the oldest children from each suite to get together to use their budding imaginations and emerging motor skills, while the infants, toddlers, and twos can enjoy a quieter morning with their primary caregiver.

For this reason, many mixed-age LifeWays programs offer a time of preschool enrichment. At the LifeWays centers in the Milwaukee area, we met this need by offering KinderHouse, a traditional Waldorf mixed-age preschool program based upon the importance of movement, play, and fantasy for the young child.

The KinderHouse children play circle games and explore language through songs and poems. They dress up to become kings and queens, mothers and fathers, or other characters inspired by the stories brought to them by

their teacher. They paint, color, enjoy puppet plays, grind grain, bake bread, make soup, model beeswax, and play outdoors in nature all while learning to play together. Time spent exploring the world in this active and creative way gives children the experiences they need to build a healthy foundation for future academic learning. KinderHouse meets for two mornings per week, from 9 AM–11:30 AM from Labor Day to Memorial Day.

What Is LifeWays Parenting?

BY CYNTHIA ALDINGER

This is a very short section, not because parenting is less important than professional caregiving! It is short because we believe in supporting parents' trust in themselves over and above advice we can offer. While there are countless parenting books on the market, we encourage you to dedicate yourself to understanding the script that is your own child.

There is no template for parenting. LifeWays Principles and Practices are intended to be applicable to both child care and parenting, and we encour-

age you to work as consciously as possible with the living arts in a form that is unique to your individual family.

Perhaps as you read Marie's story you can imagine most of those activities in your own family home with your own children. Maybe you want to read it again with that in mind!

The most important thing is this—whatever you do, do it with as much interest and joy as you can muster. Could you wish for anything more wonderful for your children to imitate and develop in their lives than interest and joy? That is why we ended Marie's story with a big *Yes!*

As we are trying to make it possible for more children to have the daily life experiences of healthy home life, you can see from our mission statement below that parents are our main inspiration! Thank you!

Mission Statement: LifeWays North America, Inc. is devoted to healthy child care practices, parent-child programs, and training programs for caregivers, nannies, parents, home-based preschool teachers, after-school care providers, and parent educators. These activities are inspired by the educational works of Rudolf Steiner and are supported by contemporary early childhood research as well as common sense and wisdom of many generations of parents.

Home Away from Home—
Rhythms, Routines, and
the Living Arts

BY CYNTHIA ALDINGER

Wash on Monday
Iron on Tuesday
Mend on Wednesday
Churn on Thursday
Clean on Friday
Bake on Saturday
Rest on Sunday

—Old Nursery Rhyme

Rhythms and Routines

Those were the days, my friend. Or were they? This little nursery rhyme heralds a time long past when what happened inside the household happened through the labor of human hands with minimal mechanical support. Most often it was the homemakers—the mothers, daughters, and grandmothers—who were in charge of these activities while the fathers, sons, and grandfathers were out in the fields engaged in equally important work.

Daily and weekly routines were adhered to relatively strictly. Making the food and tending to material things required planning and gathering of the necessary tools or ingredients. There were no 24-hour convenience stores or

even preplucked chickens! The daily routines supported the weekly rhythms, which gradually shifted according to seasonal restrictions or needs. Like a piece of classical music, the household worked best when everything was well orchestrated. Each person had a contribution to make, and as soon as children were capable, they participated. By evening time, a family meal, perhaps followed by a little music or reading and a good night's rest, were the natural finale to a full-on day of work and play.

According to Laura Ingalls Wilder's testaments to these bygone days, when children were not in school, they were helping with daily chores. When time allowed, they played with siblings or friends. Sometimes they played games to test their physical dexterity, but their "make-believe" play centered around activities of everyday life. My mother, who grew up decades after the *Little House on the Prairie* days, still recalls playing "house" by drawing a frame in the dirt with a stick. Lines were drawn to indicate the different rooms, and it was clearly understood what activities took place in each of those "rooms."

As an historical context, it is helpful and interesting to note from whence we have come in regards to homemaking and the roles children played. However, rather than sometimes feeling nostalgia for what we perceive to have been simpler times, let us consider, instead, how daily life activities, particularly those associated with homemaking, prepare our children for modern, contemporary living and create a solid foundation for lifelong learning. Before getting specific, let's look more generally at how having rhythms and routines can create a framework for healthy brain development.

We know that a child's brain is not a blank slate when he or she is born— for example, repetitive sounds in the womb already establish recognition in the baby after birth. The baby will turn its head when it hears a voice that it regularly heard before birth. Synaptic connections in the brain already exist for recognizing those sounds. Repetition is the major tool for teaching a child anything. Exposure to an experience may create a synaptic connection, but it is repetition that myelinates the pathways to that connection. Myelin is a dielectric (electrically insulating) material that forms a layer, the myelin sheath, around the axon of a neuron. Without myelination, a synaptic connection will eventually diffuse and disappear altogether due to weakness created by a lack of continued exposure to the experience. If I only play a

game one time or only fold the laundry infrequently in the presence of a young child, the capacity to remember that is limited. Frequent exposure is what imprints the brain and creates learning.

When this understanding of brain development burst onto the scene of child development, some people became excited and took it to mean that we should expose young children to a multitude of educational materials so their brains would be filled with the knowledge of abstract concepts connected to reading and math skills. Learning toys and videos for infants and toddlers were convincingly advertised as helpful tools for fast-tracking children, and numerous curricula were developed to teach very young children skills that had once been reserved for elementary school.

What was seemingly overlooked in this frenzy of edutainment was the fundamental understanding of how young children thrive. Young children, we all know, are primarily sensory beings—they want to take in the world through bodily experience, not through abstract concepts. Babies want to taste and touch every object, not just see it with their eyes. Their innate drive is to enter fully into whatever surrounds them and to have as many of their senses involved as possible.

Imagine the difference in being shown a one-dimensional card with a big red square on it to learn the concept "red" as compared to sitting near an adult who is sorting napkins or towels by color or putting a bunch of red apples into a bowl or slicing strawberries into a salad. These are all activities in which the child can participate, either actively or just by being in the presence of what is happening.

Consider the experience of putting ingredients into a bowl—adding two cups of this, a teaspoon of that, two-and-a-half tablespoons of something else, cracking and adding three eggs, mixing it all together, pouring it into a baking dish, putting it into the oven, waiting for a certain amount of time to pass on the timer, taking it out of the warm oven, waiting for it to cool before slicing it into eight pieces, and finally eating it. There is the chance to feel, smell, and taste the ingredients; hear the mixing sounds; experience the warmth of the oven; play in the water while cleaning up; sweep up whatever fell on the floor; smell the scent of what is baking; and at last taste the final product. Compare that to sorting a bunch of beans into piles with various

place values and never even getting to cook and eat them. Either way, the child may learn some foundational math concepts, but which one most appeals to the natural learning style of young children?

What is happening when a child accomplishes the skill of squeezing out just the right amount of toothpaste on the toothbrush or pouring a cup of milk without spilling it over the top or going to the grocery store and helping to put groceries into the cart with self-control, learning he cannot have every single thing he desires?

These multisensory experiences stand head and shoulders above activities geared purely to teach abstract concepts. Just as important as involving several senses is meeting the child's need to experience activities repeatedly and routinely. In this way not only are the brain connections myelinated, we also meet in a healthy way the developmental needs of the child to touch, taste, smell, see, listen, move, experience connection, and feel a bond to an attentive adult doing meaningful activities.

According to an article on brain development by Rosenberg and Reibstein in a special edition of *Newsweek*, Spring/Summer 1997:

Short of being raised in isolation, a baby will encounter enough stimulation in most households to do the trick...anything from banging pots and pans together to speaking to a sibling. The key phrase here is "properly stimulated," which is not the same as expensively stimulated or the worse fate, overstimulated.

So, how can we relate this to the times in which we are living? With modern technology, we are not required to do the household labor we had to do in the past. We don't have to cook, so why would the baby even be playing with pots and pans?

Let's press Pause for a moment. We can head down the "modern life is not good for children" route, or we can take the higher road of gratitude for what we have while considering what from earlier times is still valid for everyday life. LifeWays promotes an approach to life that embraces modern living while at the same time recognizing the gifts that simplicity, regularity, predictability, and hands-on experiences provide young children and families.

With technology creating opportunities for adults to spend less time doing household chores and more time pursuing personal interests or longer work schedules, where does that leave young children, who learn primarily by imitation and sensory experience? Common play themes observed in early childhood programs include children pretending to be talking on cell phones or sitting at computers, along with imitating television or movie characters. Imitation of life activities such as cooking, baking, cleaning, repairing, building and making things, gardening, doing laundry, car repair, caring for animals, and such are diminishing.

We could decide that is okay. However, we could also ask ourselves if we want our children to grow up without a deep sense of sustainable living. It is one type of skill to know how to open a package and put the food in the microwave, and it is another capacity to know how to crack an egg into a pan or make a sandwich or chop vegetables. It is one type of skill to remember to put your dirty laundry into the laundry basket so that someone will take care of it and have it show up clean again one day. It is another capacity to learn how to sort clothes, load a washing machine and dryer, sort and fold again, and put away clean laundry. It is one type of skill to know where to throw away broken things. It is another to experience how some things can be repaired.

There is such value for children to follow any process from beginning to end. For example, if it is possible for them to gather ears of corn from a nearby field, shuck and dry it, put the kernels in a grain mill, work so hard to grind it, make it into corn bread, and savor the results, their relationship to that corn bread is entirely different from eating it ready-made from a package.

It also seems wise for our children to know how to navigate the world in which they live and to be prepared for living in a world in which electricity and other technology sometimes fail. There are also qualitative differences in the physical gestures a child experiences when something has been lovingly tended or created by a caring adult and the gesture of pushing buttons and flipping switches to make life work.

Consider the exponential increase in childhood asthma and diabetes, social-emotional challenges, allergies, obesity, decreased attention span, and behavioral issues that are showing up in children under the age of six now. It is essential not to simplistically state that these phenomena are singularly related to the change in lifestyle over the past several decades. We want to be respectful of the individual child and family dealing with such concerns, and we acknowledge that many factors can be at play in a particular situation. However, we do not want to stick our heads in the sand and think that we can continue blithely on without taking note of the fundamental needs of our young children.

I am not proposing that all fun ends as soon as you have children and only starts up again after they get through early childhood! This is why I encourage families and caregivers to create support communities. As adults, it is our prerogative to love the unpredictable, enjoy late-night celebrating or eating junk food, watch movies or television or play video and computer games—or to prefer to read all day or spend endless hours talking on the phone or computer with friends. These are all choices that we as adults are free to make.

We need to understand, however, that these are things that are not suitable for young children. Because children are relatively malleable, they will make adjustments to accommodate whatever lifestyle surrounds them. But at what price when we consider the increase in illnesses mentioned above? Children tend to flourish in environments that are predictable with regular rhythms for eating and sleeping, playing inside and outside, and with routines that support their bodily habits such as bathing, toothbrushing, preparing for bed, and so forth. Actually, we adults also tend to be healthier when our lives have strong rhythms, particularly around food and sleep.

Occasional changes in routine, of course, are to be expected. Children thrive in the presence of adults who are happily enjoying themselves and one another at special celebratory events. When one of my favorite young caregivers got married, all the children in her care came to the wedding and danced the night away with their parents. Our sons could count on two really late nights a year when they were young—New Year's Eve and St. John's Tide (June 25). And who hasn't indulged in some tummy-upsetting food at

one or another family gathering? The important thing is for the adults to understand that the fussy behavior their children may demonstrate the next day is probably not because they are purposefully misbehaving, but because they are off-balance from the extra stimulation and change in rhythms and routines. Knowing this can help the adults make wise decisions about getting back into routine as soon as possible for the sake of their children. I have often contended that life is richer when chaos is occasional rather than a lifestyle.

Does this understanding of how children learn through imitation and movement mean that we must always be in movement around our children? Will they come to harm if we check our e-mail twice a day for a few minutes or read a chapter in our favorite book (good luck on that!) or pay our bills or any other activity that appears to be more sedentary? Don't we also want them to see us relaxing, being still sometimes or demonstrating the appropriate use of technology? It seems reasonable, particularly if we can demonstrate the ability to use technology in a brief, timely way rather than spend endless hours in front of a screen.

If any type of activity is out of balance in our lives (too much chaos or too much inactivity), it can also throw our children out of balance. They thrive on seeing us doing meaningful, creative things. Why do you think many children love watching people engaged in manual labor? They love seeing physical activity, and they can actually see how the material world changes. I have often spoken about my favorite teacher when I was a young girl in elementary school. I describe his teaching tools as things such as brooms, mops, ladders, hammers, and screwdrivers. Have you figured it out? He was our school custodian. His name was Orville Todd, or Mr. Todd to me. In our child care homes and centers, if any repairs need to be done, we try to do them when the children are present rather than after they have gone home. And if a repair person comes, he or she is warmly embraced by the children.

Even though this book is not a book on child development, it is worth noting once again that young children learn primarily through imitation. They imitate *everything*, and the sensory impressions that we provide for them—including our inner attitudes—determine what they are going to imitate. It is worth noting that sometimes it is our concentration that they im-

itate. For example, I have observed some of the deepest play in children when
they were around an adult who was fully engaged in her work, perhaps knitting or folding laundry or paying bills. Her deep concentration supported
the children's deep concentration in their play. They were not necessarily imitating her activity at the time, but her concentration created a nonchaotic
mood through which they could fully enter into their own play theme, such as
pretend grocery shopping, taking care of a baby, or building a bridge.

Children have innate drives toward certain developmental steps. But
without human beings to imitate, they only develop so far. Did you ever hear

reports of the famous wolf children who were found after having been raised by a family of wolves? The children could not speak or stand upright. They needed human models to be able to do that. Like Barbra Streisand sings, "People who need people are the luckiest people in the world!" That's all of us!

So where were we? Oh yes, we had just Paused to consider the importance of embracing the times in which we live while learning how to create anew the simplicity in which the young child thrives. So, how did we get so far away from valuing the tasks of making a home in the first place?

Let's leave behind the *Little House on the Prairie* days we started with and Fast Forward from the late nineteenth and early twentieth centuries to the 1950s. In LifeWays training classes we share a document reportedly taken from a 1950s home economics textbook on how to be a good housewife. Our twenty-first century students squirm at the suggestions for a woman to stifle herself in complete service to the comfort and delight of the man of the house. The post-1960s woman can hardly believe what she is reading. Our male students sometimes find it amusing but are equally surprised and non supportive of the proposed servitude of the wife and mother. When we take a closer look at some of the things proposed in that document—have a nice meal ready, tidy the house—we realize that these are things that benefit the whole family. As an exercise, we reinvented the document by inserting the word "family" wherever it said "husband" and found that many of the suggested activities were worthwhile and valid for creating a healthy home life. That is not to say that it is invalid to care for one's spouse. There is more of an expectation today, however, of shared responsibility in creating and maintaining a home.

The children are best served when they also share in these household responsibilities. A favorite book of mine is *The Ordinary is Extraordinary*, by Amy Laura Dombro and Leah Wallach, first published in 1988. Here is an excerpt:

These everyday activities are not just necessities that keep you from serious child rearing; they are the best opportunities for learning you can give your child and the most important time you can spend with her, because her chief task in her first three years is precisely to gain command of the day-to-day life you take for granted. Ordinary time is "quality time" too....

To a small child, our chores are intriguing performances: fresh, complex, and absorbing. For children, the mundane is new, unclassified territory, and it's magical. They set about exploring every day by collecting, organizing, and reorganizing information about their bodies and their environment, about people and how people behave and communicate with one another. To learn, they need practice. Routines give them the opportunity to observe the same sights, sounds, smells, and behaviors until they make sense of them: to make the same movements until they can coordinate confidently; to hear and use the same words until they can take possession of them.

Let's Fast Forward again.

Here we are in the twenty-first century. Both women and men in the Western world are active in all professions and walks of life. Parents and grandparents are often working outside of the home. In many homes, the practical life activities that "make it all work" happen when the children are not there or after they have gone to bed. Some families have hired services to take care of the cleaning and care of the house while no one is home, and many parents who work all day wait until they have kissed their children good night before tackling the laundry or the dishes. Meals are often picked up on the way home or eaten out. There are whole communities of children who think that food comes from the grocery store or restaurant. They are completely unfamiliar with gardens or farmer's markets.

In families where one or both parents stay at home or work from home, it *may* be that the children are more familiar with practical everyday-life activities, but not necessarily. We live in an age where child "enrichment" is rampant. Children are enrolled in multiple programs that take them out of the home starting at younger and younger ages, and schools and early childhood centers offer all-day "school" programs for the barely-out-of-diapers set.

Many infants and toddlers are also in all-day programs.

The majority of programs offered to young children are in institutional settings that have very little resemblance to a home. Track lighting, institutional furniture, washable surfaces, and plastic equipment and toys dominate the environment. Activities are typically constructed around learning outcomes and expectations for each stage of development. Preacademic learning that once took place at home through practical life activities is now offered through the use of curricula that are somewhat abstract and contrived.

Typically, all-day programs for children are set up so that only same-age children are together. Two-year-olds spend their days surrounded by other two-year-olds, infants with other infants, toddlers with toddlers. The experience of the natural unfolding of life is not visible to them. In a family home with several children, with the exception of those homes comprised of quadruplets or quintuplets, the children grow up experiencing older and younger siblings or cousins in their various stages of ability. The two-year-old aspires to the capacities of the four-year-old. The five-year-old experiences how her infant brother requires complete care and tending and is witness to how a human being grows from being a helpless horizontal baby to a walking, talking, socializing person.

When we brought our second son home from the hospital, his two-year-old brother was expecting us to bring home a playmate. "Can he get down?" was his first question. In his own dawning consciousness, he experienced that his brother had to spend a long time sleeping, eating, and growing before there would be any rolling on the floor together. He witnessed the gentle handling, the bathing, the feeding, the stages of movement. At the same time he was going through his own stages of development, which now included awakened capacities for nurturing. When, as a four-year-old, his two-year-old brother could "play" with him, there were deeper layers to the relationship. While feeling frustrated with the interference/destruction his brother brought to some of his play themes, there was also a sense of protection toward him. For the little one, there was the joy of having a slightly older model of human development in his daily life, providing capacities to aspire toward.

Please do not get the impression that all was easy, copasetic, calm, and endearing! Some things were done very well; others, half-baked. We lived in

a real household with real life stuff, with the wide range of emotions that exists when several people live together. It is called the school of life!

Now comes the question: How does the "school of life" happen when children are in early childhood settings or programs that do not include the practical life activities and the mixing of ages normally found in home life? This question is fundamental to the principles and practices we have developed for LifeWays over the years and which you were able to read about in Chapter 1.

In the LifeWays training courses and seminars, we go into more detail than we can cover in this book, but the foundation from which we teach is called the Living Arts. These refer to the arts of domestic activity, nurturing care, creative arts and crafting, and social ability. And we work individually to discover our own best form and content for a daily/weekly/seasonal life schedule that supports the health of the children in our care and supports our own continuously unfolding self as well. You can see a chart of these living arts at the end of this chapter. It was developed over a few years by workshop participants and students who were asked to list everything they could think of in each category. Clearly it is not a definitive list, and each student works to personalize it in the training courses.

Developing routines and rhythms that are practical and also enlivening is a worthy goal and like nectar for our growing children and for us. As the LifeWays training students, both professionals and parents, create their schedules, they include everything they can think of that needs to happen and that they want to happen. We encourage them to think of their life as a whole rather than compartmentalized. For example, a caregiver is not only supposed to list the things she or he does during the hours at work, but to create a chart for the whole day, the whole week, and so forth, from waking in the morning to going to bed at night.

After having heard too many caregivers and teachers over the years say "My work is interfering with my life," I realized how easy it is for people to start to feel unbalanced and resentful when there is not a flow. Particularly for individuals working with young children, it is important for them to want to be there. We discovered little things along the way. It is important for the children to experience us engaged in meaningful activity. Once we have tended the immediate physical environment we are in with the children, there

is no reason why we cannot do things that also serve our personal home lives. For example, one caregiver discovered she could do some personal mending while the children in her care were playing. Another bakes her family's birthday cakes with her child care children. Some occasionally get a jump-start on their family dinner preparations.

If you are caring for children in your home, then it is even easier to blend your professional and private lives. No harm comes to children watching their caregiver sit down for a few minutes to pay bills or write a birthday card to a friend or soak her own feet for a few minutes! It is all about balance, and one of the things that has gotten out of balance is the amount of time dedicated in our culture to entertaining and "busying" young children. We set them up for disappointment and hard times when they think that life is all about adults serving them, or when we expect them to do curricular things that are not developmentally appropriate. Let us love them with equal measures of tender loving care and benign disinterest.

What?! Am I advocating that we become disinterested in our children? Read the word before that—*benign*. It is not a disinterest that in any way harms them; rather, it frees them to explore the world without a sense that we are constantly hovering. Think of the scientist on the brink of discovery who is interrupted by some unthinking person popping into the lab and asking questions about what she is looking at under the microscope. It totally breaks her concentration! This is done far too often to the young child who has an innate need just to "be" and discover. Young children want to drink in our every move and word, but they do not want to be drowned by an overabundance directed toward them.

Benign disinterest is *not* "not knowing where the children are or what they are doing." It is being occupied with other things in such a way that they do not feel themselves being observed or noticed. Here is a wonderful passage from *The Tender Land* in which Kathleen Finneran describes her mother:

> As a child, whenever I saw her sitting at the kitchen table with the bills spread out around her, I knew I could sit right next to her and never be noticed. Instead of being bothered by her inattention, I felt calmed by it. Sitting beside her, unacknowledged, I felt as if I were in some special zone, a quiet, impenetrable place she had created with

her concentration. . . . And so I sat beside her, happy to be enveloped in her disregard, the suspension of time that came with it. . . . Did she know how soothing she could be, how she could shrink the world down to this for me?

Environments

When we consider establishing rhythms and routines that support the living arts and the daily life schedules we desire for ourselves and the children, these considerations help us to imagine the kind of environment we want to have in our home or our child care center. We want places where we can engage easily in domestic activities, where it is easy to offer nurturing care, where we can make good food, where children can play alone or in groups, where the adults can relax and tend to the things of their lives, where we can grow a garden and find ready access to an outdoor play space that supports exploration and wonder.

In other words, we want places that feel like home. The choices of furniture, lighting, equipment, toys, bedding, kitchen and dining setup are all meant to create a feeling of home, not institution.

Indoor Environments

We sense how nice it is for the children to be in a real home environment. Even in child care settings that are not actual homes, we encourage the caregivers to decorate their rooms with art and personal photographs that have meaning for them yet are also appropriate for the children in their care to see. Far too often we see children surrounded by environments that are institutional and that also have only child-oriented décor, such as Disney prints or silly motifs, or walls plastered with the children's artwork. Although this might be okay for programs that are only a couple of hours a day, such as a play school, it seems inappropriate for children who are in the environment for most of the day. What speaks to them of "home" if they are in institutional, overstimulating environments all day and in their parental home environment only nights and weekends? Certainly when my mother took care of other people's children when I was growing up, she did not change our home around to look like some sort of amusement center.

In the LifeWays training, we consider some specific things that support healthy, homelike environments for children. Mary writes about a few of them here:

> If you are caring for children in your home, you have a real advantage when creating a homelike environment. You're already there! Sometimes home child care providers, in order to meet some unspoken standard of professionalism or child development expectations, will try to create a child care center environment in their home by bringing in cubby wall systems and setting up rooms filled with learning materials, toys and furniture all scaled for children. This is not only unnecessary but also ill-advised. How many homes do you know of that look like a child care center? Your big advantage in creating a

homelike care environment for children is that you are already in a home, so don't waste that opportunity by institutionalizing your space.

You may decide that some rooms are off-limits to child care children. In my home daycare, the children had free use of the whole house except my sons' bedroom. While my sons were away during the day at school, the door to their room remained closed. Often, when the boys returned from school, they would invite the younger children in to their room to see their hamster, play a game, or see their cool rock collection; but it was at the boys' discretion. It's important that your own children feel they have some space that is not community property.

Aside from those restricted spaces, though, try to make sure the children you are caring for have use of as much of the main living space as possible, especially the kitchen. We all know that this is where the "real life" in a home usually happens. It seems that whenever my husband and I host a gathering at our home, despite all my attempts to set up a welcoming environment in the dining room or living room for the guests, they all end up crammed into our little kitchen while I'm trying to finish up the dinner preparations! Have you ever noticed this? I think it's because we, as humans, want to be where real life is happening. The same is true for children. They want to be with you as you prepare lunch, fold laundry, and sweep the floor.

Keeping a homelike environment with an emphasis on the domestic arts was really natural in my home daycare. When the time came to open the LifeWays center in Milwaukee, the space we found was perfect in terms of location and beautiful outdoor setting, but the inside space made my heart sink. It was very institutional, with squared-off classrooms attached to a huge common space, restrictions by the church on the types of furniture we could bring in, stacks and stacks of tables and chairs lining the walls for church use. How in the world would we make this space homelike?

Over the years, we've learned a lot by trial and error, and through plenty of good-natured negotiations with our landlord! There are many things that we would do differently with our space if we didn't have to take everything down on the weekends or share the space with the church. But we couldn't afford a space like this all to our-

selves, so we make do with what we have. Over the years, I've come to believe that sharing the space has other advantages, though, besides just the financial ones. By having to move every single item twice a week (once to set up on Mondays and once to take down on Fridays) we definitely don't accumulate too many things. If an item isn't getting used, it goes into storage or gets donated to charity. I've been to many child care programs that are cluttered with way too many toys, books, furniture, and other items. I'm grateful for our built-in "purging system."

From an environmental perspective, it doesn't make sense to me that many buildings are used only Monday through Friday, or others only on the weekends. From that standpoint, a child care program sharing a building with a church is a great collaborative use of space. The times the church needs their building—on the weekends and weeknights—is exactly when we don't need it. Finally, sharing space has made all of us more creative, more flexible and has opened the door to collaboration that otherwise wouldn't have happened between the church community and the LifeWays community.

So, how have we made an institutional space as homelike as possible? Here are some things we've learned:

- **We use natural and lamp lighting.** The overhead florescent lighting found in most commercial buildings is harsh, often accompanied by a buzzing sound when you turn it on. As adults, we may not even notice the effects of these lights on us, but they have a great effect on children.

  When we moved into the church building, right away we decided not to use the overhead lights in the suites but to set up lamp lighting instead. However, the main gathering room, where the children ate their lunch and got ready to go outside, was so large, we thought we had no other option than to use the overhead lighting. We began to notice that infants who were quite happy in the suite would begin to fuss as they were carried into the room with the overhead lighting. Finally, we invested in a series of floor lamps that lined the walls, providing enough light that we could turn off the overhead lights. Immediately, the demeanor of the children in that space changed, and the infants were more content. As an aside, I noticed that the headaches I routinely had been getting after a day at work (my desk is

in the gathering room) went away! Because so many of us had become accustomed to the harsh, bright lighting, it took us a while to adjust ourselves to the natural and lamp lighting. We educated the parents on the benefits of using natural lighting over commercial lighting, and very quickly we all adjusted nicely to the new, healthier light levels.

- **We paint the rooms a warm color.** Big square rooms can feel really institutional with stark white walls. So in both of our centers in the Milwaukee area, we negotiated with the landlords that we could paint our rooms a warmer color. Ideally, for the very young child, this would be a soft peach blossom color. A creamy butter yellow will also work nicely to soften a room and is often preferred by adult land-lords, who may think that peach blossom is too "pink."

- **We soften the rooms with homelike elements.** A big, comfy couch is always helpful to create a homelike space where children can cuddle

up with a caregiver to look at a book or rest quietly for a few moments. Area rugs are another way to soften a "hard" space, and curtains go a long way toward warming up an otherwise squared-off commercial window. Tablecloths and flowers make institutional-style folding tables look much more inviting. Long pieces of gossamer silk or cotton can be suspended from the ceiling and draped over a wooden play stand to create separate spaces in an otherwise vacuous room. Furniture can also be arranged into smaller groupings to divide a big room into different spaces. Dressers for the children's clothing are much more homelike than child care cubby systems.

- **We emphasize natural materials and fibers.** One of the things parents notice almost immediately upon entering a LifeWays suite is that our toys are made of natural materials and offer open-ended play. Each suite has a small wooden play kitchen area that is often the most popular play space. Toddlers appreciate having a few wooden

pretend food items in the kitchen while the four- and five-year old children can "imagine" their food from pinecones, polished rocks, shiny chestnuts, and other items from nature. Natural fiber dolls in baskets or cradles allow children to imitate the adult's care of the baby in the suite. A basket of silk squares offers hours of imaginative play, as the silks can become a cape for a prince, a dress for a queen, a leash for a dog, or a tent when draped over two play stands. And tucked into each child's drawer you'll often find a "sleeping dolly" to cuddle with at nap time each day that was made especially for him by his caregiver.

- **We use essential oils.** Our sense of smell strongly affects how we perceive the space we are in. We often use essential oils diffused into the air to bring a homier, calmer feel to our child care suites. Lavender oil is the clear favorite, as it is calming and has antiseptic qualities.

- **We do domestic work.** We've found that the best way to make a space more homelike is to bring more home life to it. When I walk into Life-Ways in the morning and see a small group of children helping their caregiver fold yesterday's laundry, while another caregiver is taking a delicious-smelling pan of baked oatmeal out of the oven for morning snack, I think I'm home!

Outdoor Environments

Just recently I came across a blog called Free Range Kids and was inspired by the writing of Lenore Skenazy, who recognizes the importance of children playing outside without the feeling of constant supervision or adult-guided play. In licensed child care, of course, we must establish safe outdoor play environments, and we may find ourselves needing to put on our children's-advocate hats. The first center in which I worked was able to license our backyard tree as a piece of climbing equipment. We were required to put wood chips beneath it, but that felt like a small compromise in order to preserve our children's right to climb trees.

In establishing backyard environments, consider the possibility of bushes, trees, or even a small building structure in which the children can sense that clubhouse feeling of closeness. Later in this chapter you will find a list of other ideas to inspire creative outdoor environments and experiences.

Fortunately there is a growing body of research upholding the awareness that children tend to thrive in nature. Richard Louv's book *Last Child in the Woods* has reawakened this awareness to the extent that spending time in nature is now considered therapeutic activity for children with a variety of challenges. My own experience with children exposed to screen time (television, video games, computers) is that nature can help to heal the negative impact the screen time has on them. It requires a commitment on the part of the adults, however, to be sure the nature experiences are available to the children in their care and that there is at least a 2:1 or even a 3:1 ratio of nature time to screen time (e.g., two or three hours of nature time to one hour of screen time).

If a child gets home from school at 3:30 PM and is going to be in bed by 7:30 PM and have an hour devoted to eating and preparing for sleep, that leaves about three hours in the afternoon. This tells me that it is probably best to leave any screen time to the weekends when there is more time to offer the therapeutic nature time to counterbalance it. If a family has Friday night movie night, for example, and the children are allowed two hours of other screen time over the weekend, they would want to be sure the children had at least ten hours of nature time also. That could look like an hour of outdoor playtime each weekday and five hours of outdoor playtime over the weekend.

I discovered this ratio when I was a kindergarten teacher and had wonderful conversations with a father of three children for whom I was their teacher. In a warm and friendly manner, we would banter back and forth regarding my desire for his children to have less exposure to television and movies and his retort to look at his children and see how balanced they were. How could I argue with him when they were indeed three of the most peaceful children in my kindergarten over the years. One thing I noticed was that, rather than screen time ramping them up and making them hyperactive (what I usually noticed in children), his children tended to be more lethargic and tired after they experienced screen time. Still, they were basically very happy, balanced children. After puzzling over this for months, I realized that these children spent a large amount of time with their father in nature— hiking, fishing, and working in the garden. Taking note of this, I starting

noticing this with other children and was delighted when Louv came out with his book corroborating the healing effects of nature.

In the meantime, even the American Academy of Pediatrics urges parents not to expose children under two to screen time, and there is a growing recognition that it is best for all children, especially those under seven, to have limited exposure. Interesting, isn't it, that in this section on nature, we ended up considering screen time! I think that is because we are seeing less and less children outside—with the exception of organized sports—due to the fact that they are inside on computers and in front of televisions. Our resolution in LifeWays homes and centers is not to have any screen time.

Children in our LifeWays settings go outside every day with few exceptions. Mary O'Connell tells of one day when their licensing specialist visited on a snowy day in Milwaukee and was surprised to find all of the children at the center outside playing. He was very pleased yet admitted that this was the only center he had visited that day in which the children had gone outside.

Why is nature experience so important? If we revisit our awareness that young children learn through sensory experience and the ability to move their bodies, there are few places that provide such a variety of experience as natural environments. The more they are allowed to do their climbing, slithering, rolling, shouting, running, tunneling, hiding, digging, and exploring in nature, the more we are free to create really homelike indoor environments rather than curricular-driven indoor play gyms.

Another valuable outdoor experience is the neighborhood walk, where the children can get a feel for the life of the neighborhood—Mrs. A's lovely garden, Mr. B's new sidewalk, Ms. C's dog who always comes out to greet and meet. I love a photograph I have in which Mary and the children in her home program were on a neighborhood walk. The photo was taken by a school crossing guard who had come to know them because of the regularity of their walks. He had become an extension of their child care *family*. Being outside, being in nature, has a way of helping us feel more expansive, not only to wonders and glories of the natural world, but also to one another.

One further word on the outdoor environments is a word of encouragement to seek places, whenever possible, that are not overly cultivated. Louv has indicated that the wilder or *greener* the space, the more therapeutic it is

for children. From backyard to playground to forest, the level of health-restoring properties increases proportionally to the level of uncultivated nature. Finding such places is not always possible, particularly if you are in the city. In that case, it might be worthwhile to consider having an area in the yard that has tall grasses and wildflowers, for example, or some areas where the children can feel they are hidden away, even though the caregivers know at all times where they are.

There is no truer science curriculum for young children than giving them the opportunity to experience and explore. It is not about offering theory and facts to what it is that they observe. Is it about leaving them free in the experience that nature speaks to them. In this way, when they grow older, their sense of wonder as a child can metamorphose into a sense of responsibility and interest in the world around them. Rachel Carson, the mother of the environmental movement and author of *Silent Spring*, wrote:

> *If facts are the seeds that later produce knowledge and wisdom, then the emotions and the impressions of the senses are the fertile soil in which the seeds must grow.*

Essentials for Indoor Environments

- Open spaces—circular
- Contained places
  - secret places, nooks & crannies, pantries, cabinets
  - fort possibilities (couch cushions or a sheet over a table, for example)
- Age-appropriate toys—not too many
- Varied gradations—possibility for toddlers to climb
- Homelike furniture—for example, chests of drawers rather than cubbies, couch, etc.
- Protected place for nonambulatory infants
- Pull-up and walking space for toddlers

- Sensory variations—variety of natural materials, fabrics, colors, good smells, tasty food, for example
- Smooth surfaces, rough surfaces
- Light things (pillows), heavy things
- Hard things, soft things
- Body care essentials
- Bathrooms that feel welcoming for toilet training
- Indirect lighting (lamps and natural lighting whenever possible)
- Organized and delineated areas—e.g., this is where folding laundry happens, ironing happens; where food preparation happens, mealtime happens; where changing clothes happens, brushing teeth, cooking; where we always feed the baby, etc.
- Fresh air
- Nurturing furniture—rocking chair—furniture that hugs
- Room for large motor activity
- Beautiful place for sleeping
- Safe places for various products—even organic cleaning products
- Cleaning supplies and equipment that welcome child's participation if interested
- Artistic coloring, wall hangings, sculptures—not just children's art
- Items that are meaningful to the adults—bookshelves, telescope, hobby supplies—but that are protected from children hurting themselves or hurting the equipment
- Embracing architecture
- Magic/Wonder—special things such as a button box or a beautiful sewing box or healing basket
- Tidy but not pristine atmosphere

Essentials for Outdoor Environments

- Open areas
- Contained areas—for hiding, feeling unwatched—such as bushes, low trees

- Secret places/hiding places
- Varied gradations—small hill of dirt, sand, or stones, for example
- Flat area for laying down a blanket for babies to lie on
- Hay or straw bales or something to create a boundary around the babies on blankets
- Hill for climbing and rolling down
- Tree stumps for moving around and climbing on
- Wood planks for children to use for building teeter-totters or other creative devices
- Garden—even if it is only a small container garden
- Lilting sound of soft chimes in the wind
- Sand
- Digging tools
- Wild spaces
- Threshold places (where there is a dramatic change from one environment to the next)
- Freedom to explore and move
- Fort-building materials
- Animals
- Willingness to allow children to freely explore once you have established that there is no life-threatening danger—poisonous snakes, spiders, or plants
- Sunny places
- Shady places

Considerations for Urban Sites

- In city locations, most of the above can be created on a small scale.
- A fenced area may be required.
- Also of value in the city are the following:
  - sidewalks—especially after a rain, when they have lots of puddles

- neighborhoods to explore
- old churches to go inside—usually peaceful and full of beautiful art
- parks—especially ones that have a treed area for playing, not just playground equipment
- graveyards—often beautiful nature spaces
- work crews repairing buildings, streets, trimming trees, etc.

Examples of the Living Arts from Daily Life

Domestic Activity

Baking	Tidying	Repairing things
Cooking	Vacuuming	Cleaning
Dishes	Setting the table	Laundry:
Sweeping	Paying bills	sorting
Dusting	Shopping	washing
Polishing	Grocery shopping	drying
Mopping	Gardening	folding
Windows	Yard maintenance	ironing
Toilets and sinks	Vehicle maintenance	putting away
Organizing	Washing vehicles	Playfulness in activities

Nurturing Care

Free play	Soothing/holding and touching	Noninterference/noninterrupting
Singing and music	Adult bodily care (e.g., massage, manicure)	Providing homelike environment
Rocking		
Bathing	Patting down for nap	Tending boo-boos
Hand washing	Oiling face after nap	Providing quiet and silence
Footbaths	Appropriate rough-housing	
Face washing		Allowing childlike noise
Hair brushing	Laughing	
Toothbrushing	Protecting child's autonomy	Storytelling
Diapering and toileting		Reading

Exercise

Water play

Blessings/prayer time/ gratitude

Adult's spiritual practice/meditation

Alone time/together time

Sick care/preventive care

Nature experiences

Creative Discovery

Creative play

Baking

Sewing

Crocheting

Knitting

Crafting

Woodworking

Painting

Modeling

Singing

Recitation

Storytelling

Puppetry

Dramatic play

Games

Decorating/flower arranging

Aesthetic care of environment

Seasonal activities

Making gifts

Social Ability

Play

Games

Circle time (age-appropriate)

Visiting friends, family, neighbors

Parties

Birthdays

Festivals

Church

Playground play

Nature play (alone or together)

Multigenerational opportunities

Mealtime

Shopping

Caring for others in need

Singing

Giving gifts

Online and other communications

Family organizational meetings

Finding Your Colleagues

BY MARY O'CONNELL

At the center of the universe is a loving heart that continues to beat and that wants the best for every person. Anything we can do to help foster the intellect and spirit and emotional growth of our fellow human beings, that is our job. Those of us who have this particular vision must continue against all odds. Life is for service.

—Fred Rogers

TO PROVIDE QUALITY CHILD CARE we must often enlist the help of other caring adults. If opening a child care center is in your plans, you'll need to think about finding the other members of your staff. Even those caregivers opening a family home child care program sometimes choose to hire an assistant to give them support and a little more freedom, and an adult colleague to combat the loneliness that can sometimes be part of a home daycare provider's life.

If you are a family child care provider and you don't feel you can afford to hire an assistant, or your state licensing regulations will not allow it, don't be afraid to think outside the box. Years ago when I had my home child care program, I faced this same situation, yet I yearned for an adult colleague in my work. After being inspired by an article in *Mothering* magazine about cre-

ating a "tribe" of support for your parenting journey, I approached a friend, a stay-at-home mother whose parenting style I not only admired, but meshed well with my own. I hesitantly suggested that one morning per week she bring her children to my house and we would bake bread together, as well as share parenting duties such as diapering, singing songs, telling stories, and more. To my great surprise, she readily accepted. In hindsight, I think she felt as isolated in her work as I felt in mine. This began what came to be called Baking Day, and it was a morning that both the children and the adults eagerly anticipated every week for more than a year.

I think a big factor in the success of our Baking Day was my initial carefulness about the person whom I invited into our home program. Finding your colleagues, whether paid or unpaid, requires some serious thought. Since the LifeWays approach to child care is relationship-based care, the adults who provide the circle of care for the child must be chosen very carefully. We know that the child learns about his world primarily through imitation of the adults who surround him. Obviously, then, the caregiver must be an adult worthy of the child's imitation. In a child care center, this also applies to the director, the cook, the cleaning person, the maintenance person, and even the bookkeeper, if they are part of the general landscape of adults who interact with the child during his day.

We have found that our best staff members have come to us through word-of-mouth recommendations by parents at the center, other staff members, or community members who know what type of program we run and what types of individuals we seek. We have, in desperate moments, run ads on the job website of the local technical college and in the local newspaper, or posted flyers on the nearby university's employment bulletin board. In general, the individuals who responded to the ads were folks who were schooled and experienced in mainstream child care (large group sizes, single-age groupings, institutional setting), and for most of them it was just too far of a stretch to embrace our philosophies and practices. We found one extraordinary caregiver this way, but we really had to kiss a lot of frogs before we found her!

So, what are the traits we look for in those adults who will be our colleagues in the care of the young child? The list that follows is a collaborative

effort of several LifeWays center directors, who have identified the characteristics present in their best caregivers. While it is not always easy to spot these qualities in a thirty-minute job interview, we can be on the lookout for certain traits as candidates talk about their past job experiences, what they're looking for in a position, and so on. One way to see if an individual exhibits the traits you're looking for is to hire him in a part-time support role, if possible. Most of our primary caregivers have begun their work at LifeWays as volunteers, substitute caregivers, part-time assistant caregivers, or cooks. This provides an opportunity to really get to know them in the environment in which they'll be working.

It is always a good idea to have a probation period for each person you hire. This is generally a six-month to one-year period of time in which you can decide if the individual is a good fit for your program. Ideally, throughout the probation period you are meeting regularly with the new employee for coaching and ongoing performance review. Then, at the end of the agreed-upon probation time, you will be able to assess the long-term future of the caregiver in your program.

Useful Places to Recruit Colleagues

- Put the word out at local Waldorf or other like-minded schools, perhaps putting something in their newsletter that goes home to parents and teachers.
- Let current or perspective parents in your program know that you are looking for a new staff member.
- Ask your current staff members if they have friends or acquaintances that might be good additions to the program.
- Contact LifeWays North America to post an employment opportunity for their training students and graduates.
- Post flyers at like-minded businesses and organizations in your neighborhood, such as the local natural foods store or La Leche League group.

Characteristics of a LifeWays Caregiver

Commitment. In *The Irreducible Needs of Children,* by Stanley Greenspan, M.D., and T. Berry Brazelton, M.D., the two child development experts outline the most basic needs of young children in order for them to grow up healthy and whole. The first irreducible need of the young child described by Greenspan and Brazelton is the need for ongoing nurturing relationships. Greenspan writes:

> The lion's share of the baby's time needs to be with caregivers who are going to be an ongoing part of the child's life and have the child's trust. The depth of one's intimacy and feelings for others depends in part on the depth of feeling one experiences in ongoing relationships.
>
> Therefore, not just any caregiver will do.... Child care arrangements where children are spending most of their day with transient caregivers should not be viewed as optimal or chosen by design.

One of his recommendations for meeting this need in child care is that the child remain with the same primary caregiver for at least the first three years of life. The primary caregiver in the LifeWays model is an individual who understands the vital role he or she plays in the child's life and is committed to staying in the position several years. If the primary caregiver will be yourself, examine honestly if you intend to make a commitment of at least three years to the care of these children.

Warmth. A basic ingredient in the caregiver-child relationship is warmth. A good caregiver shows genuine care and concern for the children in his or her care. When observing how a caregiver interacts with the children, one should see an ease and familiarity in the relationship. The child seeks the caregiver for comfort if hurt or sad, and is eager to share discoveries and thoughts. This warmth should also extend to the child's parents. The caregiver always supports the connection between the child and his parents, knowing that this is the most important relationship for the child. Caregivers who secretly or openly yearn to be the most important person in a young child's life often foster a manipulative relationship with the child that is unhealthy.

A warm relationship is one in which the caregiver shows a genuine love for the child, which is not the same as coddling. We support and encourage

the child, but not in a way that holds the child back from developing independence, taking necessary risks, or undertaking challenging tasks.

Appreciation. Childhood is an authentic time unto itself, not just a time to prepare for schooling. A good caregiver appreciates the children in his or her care as individuals who are worth getting to know. They are not simply "incomplete adults" who need to be molded in a certain way and filled up with knowledge to become productive members of society. The caregiver takes the time to get to know the child's likes, dislikes, temperament, fears, sense of humor, and other aspects of the child's unique personality.

He or she also helps the child's parents understand and celebrate the individuality of their child, while allaying common parental fears that the child isn't developing quickly enough compared to the neighbor child down the street or the development chart in the back of the parenting book. Parents

today feel so much pressure that their child achieve milestones on or ahead of schedule, so it is an essential part of the caregiver's job to share heartwarming stories that help foster a true appreciation for the child as an individual.

Joyfulness. Young children radiate joy. Often when an adult interacts with a little one, we see the adult's face soften immediately. The young child's joy is contagious. Amid the day-to-day work of caring for a group of young children, however, many adults find it difficult to maintain that joy. A caregiver who, after the third dirty diaper of the morning and countless runny noses, is able to stop and genuinely appreciate a bouquet of wilted dandelions from a sweaty, out-of-breath child, is a treasure. Indeed, the best caregivers share the child's pleasure in all of his new discoveries throughout the day, and they have

an inner joy that truly meets the wonder of the child.

Joyfulness was a characteristic I found missing in the caregivers of young children during a recent walk through a nationally accredited child care center. Teachers who were charged with the care of large groups of same-age children appeared bored and sometimes sharp-tempered with the children. The resulting effect on the children was palpable. It was as if one could see, feel, and touch the level of stress that blanketed the room. Could it be that the caregivers' lack of joy in their work was due to the fact that the expectations of their job and a lack of autonomy dampened the possibility for joy?

Recently, a LifeWays colleague who used to work at a large, well-respected child care facility shared a story about something that she had observed while working there. One morning, a caregiver in her room was folding towels while the children were playing. This was something that was supposed to be done during nap time, as the director felt it took her full attention away from watching the children; but for some reason she was doing this task in their presence. The children became interested in the laundry folding, and soon she had a group of little ones eagerly folding towels, while other children played happily nearby. The director entered the room and told the caregiver to put the laundry away until nap time. How sad that the director failed to recognize the joyful discovery and healthy interaction that was taking place!

Most people who seek to work with young children begin their career with a certain level of joyfulness. One wonders how many bored and discontented caregivers would be able to maintain this joy if they were encouraged to engage in purposeful adult work instead of stand around "watching the children" or feel bound to a curriculum that does not truly meet the developmental and playful needs of the young child.

Adaptability. Life with young children is never predictable, and while a good caregiver creates a strong and healthy schedule for the group to follow, he or she must be able to "go with the flow." I think this is one reason LifeWays caregivers often refer to the *rhythm* of the day as opposed to a mere *schedule*. Rhythm indicates a more dynamic ebb and flow of activity that adapts somewhat to the needs of the group, whereas a strict schedule can feel oppressive and rigid. The caregiver must pay attention to the needs of the group and

try to create a daily rhythm that really holds the children and provides security and comfort as they begin to know what to expect at each time of the day. But the caregiver must also be able to make changes as needed. Many congratulate themselves when they finally help their children reach a point where the daily rhythm is so strong it carries the group along throughout the day, only to have a new baby enter the mix. Anyone who has cared for an infant knows how quickly one tiny person can upset the balance of an entire household! The same is true for a group of children in child care. Illness, several days of severe weather, or an interrupted nap time can just as easily tip the scales. Adaptability is crucial.

Adaptability also refers to the capacity of the caregiver to meet the needs of the individual child while maintaining an awareness of the group as a whole. Both goals are equally important. The best caregivers develop the ability to maintain order and encourage a healthy dynamic in the group at all times while carving out moments for the one-on-one time that is so vital for each child. This is an old-fashioned skill used by mothers for centuries. It often presents a challenge for new caregivers and can take some time and experience to master.

Reverence. Often, people lament that children in our modern culture are growing up with a lack of respect for people and things. Reverence, the honoring and respecting of the divine in all things, is important to foster in early childhood. However, like many important traits, this cannot be taught through words or doctrine but must be living in the adults who are caring for the child. In her book *You Are Your Child's First Teacher,* Rahima Baldwin Dancy refers to those caring for the young child as "caretakers of the divine."

The foundation of reverence is gratitude. Does the caregiver show gratitude for those people and things around her? This will cultivate a sense of gratitude in the child. Rudolf Steiner, founder of Waldorf Education, said:

> If he sees that everyone who stands in some kind of relationship to him in the outer world shows gratitude for what he receives from this world; if, in confronting the outer world and wanting to imitate it, the child sees the kind of gestures that express gratitude, then a great deal is done towards establishing in him the right moral attitude.

The characteristic of reverence does not refer to a certain religion or spiritual practice in the adult. Many fine caregivers in LifeWays programs have come from varied spiritual paths. The common thread observed in the best caregivers is that they develop a regular spiritual practice that not only feeds their soul, but also fosters a respect for the spiritual path of the child.

Ability to work with other adults. I've heard it said by more than one caregiver, "It's not the children that are difficult to work with, it's the grown-ups!" Indeed, adult relationships can pose a challenge for many of us in our work. In child care, we interface with parents, colleagues, landlords, state licensing inspectors, and other adults on a daily basis. The ability to communicate in a healthy way with other adults is a skill that all of us continue to work on and struggle with. A good caregiver is willing to work through struggles in communication and keeps an open mind, putting him or herself in the other person's shoes.

With coworkers, a caregiver's flexibility is important. "My way or the highway" doesn't work well in most environments, especially in a small child care center where the adults are in fairly close contact all day long. Staff members must be willing to work together to create an environment where concerns can be voiced, ideas can be shared, and mistakes are forgiven. While we are all at different levels of development in terms of our ability to work with other adults, a caregiver who has serious problems communicating with colleagues will act as a type of poison in your program. An environment of gossip, polarizing into opposing groups, and avoiding one another can quickly result. It must be made clear that this type of behavior is not acceptable in an environment where we are modeling healthy relationships for children. If the staff member is not able to improve his or her adult communication skills (and ongoing conversations about this problem have been carefully documented), the end result must be dismissal.

Ongoing self-development and study. As I mentioned earlier, since the young child learns primarily through imitation, it stands to reason that the caregiver must always strive to be an adult worthy of imitation. None of us is perfect, but it is in our own striving to improve ourselves that the children in our care find the best example of what it means to be an adult. The finest LifeWays caregivers are those individuals who are not afraid to do the inner work necessary for their own self-development. This is not an easy thing, as it often leads to many questions about how we have been raised ourselves and whether we are satisfied with the behaviors we exhibit, both consciously and unconsciously. A caregiver must be open to asking herself some hard questions and striving to be more conscious in her actions.

In addition, a LifeWays caregiver must be open to ongoing study and deepening understanding of child development, from a variety of perspectives. It seems that almost daily a new study emerges that sheds new light on the needs and capacities of the young child. An interest in contemporary research, as well as continuing study of more classical works, including those of Rudolf Steiner, is evident in a good caregiver. Caregivers may or may not seek out this study material on their own, so it is important that the director or another designated colleague continue to share interesting information to promote ongoing conversation and self-study.

Good health. The daily work of caring for young children can be physically demanding and exhausting. Lifting and carrying children, bending or squatting to help with diapering, toileting, and dressing are just a few of the activities that a caregiver engages in throughout the day. A caregiver of little children is also exposed to more germs than the average person. Those adults who are in relatively good physical health are much more able to meet the demands of the job. Often, in the first year or two of working in child care, a caregiver will tend to catch every illness that the children bring into the group. Once he or she has had an opportunity to build up a healthy immunity, the frequency tends to subside. However, the overall health and vitality of the adult is an important indicator of how the caregiver responds to and recovers from these illnesses.

Interest in the domestic arts. LifeWays is a model of home, not school, so it is important that the LifeWays caregiver is open to learning and embracing the domestic arts. Many caregivers of young children today are experienced in the art projects, theme-based curriculum, and "activity centers" common in many child care programs; but very few have real life experience with or even respect for the home arts. Decades ago, children learned the arts of cooking, baking, mending, simple woodworking, and gardening in the home. When they themselves became parents or caregivers of children, these skills were passed on through the tasks of everyday living. Over time, many of these activities have disappeared from our home lives, so the adults who are entering the child care field today don't often have any life experience in these areas.

A good LifeWays caregiver may or may not have a background in the domestic arts, but must be open to learning and applying these skills in his or her work with the children. Caregivers who need to learn about the domestic arts as an adult will often find a wealth of experience in their colleagues who are already working in a LifeWays environment. The LifeWays training also teaches many of the skills necessary for a caregiver to learn how to be "at home" with the children.

As you read and reflect on the above list of attributes, you may begin to think that the caregiver you are searching for is some impossible combination of Mary Poppins and Mother Theresa. Never fear! The directors that collaborated on the above characteristics all agreed that it is the individual's openness to developing these areas that makes him an exceptional caregiver. Oftentimes, individuals will not necessarily exhibit every one of these traits, but will share an enthusiasm and a sincere effort for learning more about how to truly meet the needs of the children that encourages us to give them the opportunity to try.

Characteristics of a LifeWays Director

Many times, people interested in starting a LifeWays program are afraid that being the director requires a business background or other skills that they don't possess. In most cases, depending upon your state's licensing requirements, other individuals can be employed to fill in the gaps such as bookkeeping, administrative functions, marketing, and so on. The primary job of the director is to have a clear vision of the LifeWays principles and practices and to effectively share that vision with the rest of the staff. Thus, the two crucial characteristics of a LifeWays director are integrity and leadership.

Integrity. As a director of a small child care center, one wears many hats. On any given day, you might be meeting with prospective parents, resolving a conflict between two staff members, stepping in as a substitute caregiver, and unplugging a toilet, all before lunchtime. Amid this daily hustle and bustle, it can be difficult to remain focused on the vision of what you and your colleagues are trying to create. Often we think of integrity as coming into play when we are faced with a momentous decision. In reality, little situations present themselves many times each day that call us to reflect on our mission and respond with integrity.

Questions that seem simple enough, from how we will diaper the infants to what our policy is for children with fevers, often require much more conscious thought than we expect at first glance. Here's an example of one of the many decisions that arise daily.

We have a limit of eight children in our Forest Kindergarten program. Usually this program is full, with a waiting list of one or two children. Parents will often urge us to let their child into the program because it's "just one more child." Licensing regulations would allow us to enroll more children without adding another teacher. The extra child's tuition would definitely help the budget. And that child on the waiting list would surely benefit from the experience. But we have determined that the optimal number of children in Forest Kindergarten, for both the children and the teacher to have the most positive experience, is eight. And so the decision is made not to expand the program, even for one more child.

Decisions such as this must be made on a daily basis. When faced with a decision, even one that appears mundane on the surface, it is vital for the director to stop and ask, "Does this help us fulfill our mission?" "How does this fit with the principles and practices of LifeWays?" Of course, we must keep in mind what is reasonable, and we must live within a budget; but at no point can a LifeWays director sacrifice integrity for expediency, convenience, or economics.

Leadership. Too often, we see leadership as the ability of an individual to walk ahead of a group of people, showing them the way and getting them to follow. But I think that for the most part we travel together in a group, with our friends and colleagues beside us on our journey. True leadership demands that we call on the strengths and gifts of all of our colleagues and encourage them to share those gifts to help the whole group achieve the vision. If we have chosen the right people to help us care for the children, this task is easier than you might think.

I'd like to share a recent story from our center as an example. We had a new caregiver begin with us. She had only been with her own suite of children for a few weeks before an infant was enrolled. This caregiver had not yet had a chance to take the LifeWays training, so I decided to give her a "crash course" in how we care for infants at LifeWays. Among many things that I shared with her, I explained that we honor the philosophy developed by Dr. Emmi Pickler, the Hungarian physician who inspired the work of Magda Gerber. Most notably, the infant needs freedom of movement to develop in

the healthiest way. Therefore, we don't prop the infant in an infant seat, bouncer, swing, or other device that restricts her movement or puts her in a position she couldn't otherwise achieve on her own (obviously, a car seat while riding in the car is the exception).

When the baby's mother brought her in the first day, I noticed that she left a stroller for the caregiver that uses the car seat to hold the baby. I reminded the caregiver that we don't like to leave infants in car seats for very long, and she nodded in agreement. I saw her occasionally make use of the car seat/stroller contraption to take the baby outside with the rest of the group, but it seemed so brief a period that I didn't object. Then one day as I was doing some work in the play yard, I saw the baby "camped" in the car seat for an extended period of time. As I had already clearly explained the expectation twice, I was getting annoyed and began to conclude that the caregiver either didn't care what our philosophy was or blatantly ignored it because she didn't agree with it.

I took a moment to take a deep breath, and then I approached her, again sharing our philosophy on freedom of movement for the infant. But then something told me to really listen to this caregiver instead of just state the expectation and walk away, as I realized had been my pattern in the last two conversations. What I finally "heard" was that the caregiver was frustrated because the baby preferred the car seat, as it was what she was used to at home. When put down on her back, the baby became fussy. The caregiver also shared that we didn't have another lying-down style stroller available to use for the baby, and the ground was too wet and muddy to lay her down on a blanket. What followed was a very constructive conversation in which I was able to help the caregiver see how the baby could be helped to get used to lying on her back, and I also promised to purchase the right type of buggy within two days. Over the next week, I overheard the other caregivers initiating discussions with her about our infant practices, and some pretty great conversations ensued as they shared how they put our philosophy to work in a real-life, practical way. The caregiver seemed relieved that she finally had the tools to practice the type of infant care she hadn't known how to achieve. And I learned a valuable lesson about leadership. Walking ahead of the group, stating the goals, and expecting everyone to follow them is not true leader-

ship. We must listen to our colleagues, enlist their help, and be open to learning what they can teach us.

Characteristics of a LifeWays Cook

You may want to offer a healthy hot lunch and snacks in your child care program. If you are a family child care provider, you probably don't have the luxury of hiring a cook, so the task of preparing food will fall to you. Some child care centers have the caregivers take turns preparing the meals, but others choose to hire a cook. There are certain skills that are helpful in whoever is doing the cooking for the children.

Commitment to whole, organic foods. Cooking with whole foods from scratch is an art. It takes time and effort on the part of a cook to prepare food this way, but it is well worth the investment. There are the obvious benefits of better nutrition and reduced exposure to additives and chemicals for the children. A vast array of scientific evidence now points to the fact that whole foods, organic if possible, are healthier for children. But we can't overlook the effect of home cooking on the overall atmosphere of the center. Visitors to the center often comment on the delicious smells coming from the kitchen. Nothing says homelike care more than home-cooked food.

Commitment is key on the part of the person who is cooking. Many factors can undermine our commitment to whole, organic foods. One obstacle is the price of organic food. The child care budget is often tight, and organic food can represent a large portion of it. At our LifeWays centers, food is our largest expense after payroll. It can be tempting to purchase lower-quality foods and snacks to save money, but when we consider the ultimate cost of these foods in terms of the health of the children and the planet, it is too great a price.

Another factor that can test our commitment to whole foods cooked from scratch is the time it takes to prepare them. Even organic foods are now offered in more and more convenient forms, and this can be tempting to the cook who is short on time or the director who is attempting to reduce the number of payroll hours. But compare the experience of dumping a can of beans into a pan for warming to that of soaking the whole dried beans the

night before and slowly simmering the pot throughout the morning while adding spices to taste. Not only are the beans cooked from scratch more nutritious, but the process of the slow and meaningful food preparation done in the presence of the children nurtures them in a way that nothing else does.

A third challenge in our attempt to serve natural, whole foods is the fact that many people are unfamiliar with how to prepare them. If you are hiring someone to cook for your child care program, be very cautious about hiring the person who says she doesn't really know anything about cooking whole foods from scratch but is willing to try. In general, it is quite challenging to take up this kind of cooking; and if the commitment doesn't come from the inside, it can be difficult to maintain. It is far too easy to slip back into patterns of cooking with convenience foods when we are busy or tired. You want to search for a cook who is familiar with cooking whole foods from scratch and is eager to bring her skill and enthusiasm to your program.

If you are cooking for your own home program and are finding it challenging to stay committed to cooking whole foods from scratch, set some realistic goals for yourself and hold yourself to them. For example, when I was cooking for my own home program, I started by taking the foods I was already preparing and figuring out ways to incorporate more whole grains and fresher ingredients. Slowly, over time, I began to experiment with more time-consuming and challenging recipes, often taking the time to prepare foods on the weekends and freeze them for use during hectic days with the children. My previously mentioned Baking Day with my friend was very helpful in learning how to do some of this cooking in the presence of the children.

Timeliness and efficiency. While it's important for any employee to be on time, it is crucial for the cook to get to work in time to prepare a home-cooked meal without being rushed. The kitchen is often the central hub of a LifeWays program, and the mood in the kitchen permeates the whole center. The cook who joyfully and calmly prepares the food, chats with the children as they pass through the kitchen during the morning, and takes the time to beautifully set the table sets the mood for every child and caregiver in that space. Contrast this mood to the one set by the cook who runs in late, prepares

lunch as quickly as possible while preoccupied with other things, and does little more than "throw" the food on the table.

One LifeWays cook shared something she learned about cooking from the Lakota Indian tribe when she lived with them for a time. The Lakota believe that the emotions we feel as we are cooking actually enter the food as if they are an ingredient and are thus consumed by those who eat the meal. In honoring this belief, she made sure that she arrived at work with plenty of time to slowly prepare the children's food with intention. She tried to clear her head of distractions and negative thoughts, and focus on the preparation of the home-cooked meal.

Of course, when cooking for any large group of people, efficiency is key. The most calm and joyful cook in the world doesn't do your program much good if he or she happily produces a meal forty-five minutes past the time lunch was to have been served. When serving young children, lunch needs to be on the table promptly at noon (or whatever has been deemed lunchtime), and if it is not, the whining and fussing will definitely remind you that the meal is late.

Cleanliness. At LifeWays, our cook tends to the overall cleanliness and order of the kitchen, which is no small task considering that a number of adults and children use the space regularly throughout the day. While the children and their caregivers participate in some of the food preparation and in washing dishes after lunch, it is the cook who gives the kitchen its final touches. Our cook assumes responsibility for the general cleanliness of the common areas as well. For instance, when all the children come in from outside before lunch, their boots may occasionally end up in a somewhat disorganized heap inside the door, despite their caregiver's best efforts to encourage the children to line them up tidily. Often the person who has the time to tidy and straighten all those boots is the cook, who sweeps and washes the floor after lunch as the children settle in for their naps. It is very satisfying to see the coats, boots, hats, and mittens all straightened up in a careful manner. It sends a comforting message to both the parents and the children about the care we take of the children's belongings.

Characteristics of a LifeWays Preschool Teacher, Forest Kindergarten Teacher, or Parent-Child Group Leader

Most of the characteristics listed above for LifeWays caregivers also apply to the preschool teacher or the parent-child group leader. While the child care suite is based on the model of healthy living with children, the preschool program and the parent/child program are a bit more definitive in their scope. We want them to also reflect the qualities of a healthy home, yet they each have a specific focus as well.

The preschool teacher needs to be well versed in the various songs, games, stories, and activities that typically are experienced in a Waldorf-style preschool/kindergarten program. Of course, the primary caregivers need many of these tools as well, but they may be used slightly differently in the mixed-age child care suite. A caregiver pulls a little verse, rhyme, or song out of his pocket at any given moment as is needed. While the caregiver might also have a time of day that he does some of these things with the whole group, it is usually short and sweet due to the mixed ages. Since the preschool teacher does not have infants and toddlers along, he can slightly expand the experience for the older ones. The circle games may be a little more varied and involved, the artistic/craft activities might require more dexterity, and the stories might be a bit longer.

In LifeWays settings that do not have a separate preschool program, caregivers often wonder how to offer these more elaborate experiences for their preschool-age children when there is one adult caring for a group of children ages three months to six years. Some caregivers offer these experiences to the whole group, knowing that the little ones will participate as they are able or will play on their own while the older ones participate. In my home program, I often offered the preschoolers some of these experiences during the baby's morning nap.

The Forest Kindergarten teacher needs to be comfortable outside in nature and should love the outdoors with a bit of an adventurous spirit. Yet he or she also must understand and honor common sense safety measures and be sure to have a backpack filled with the necessary accoutrements for tending to

boo-boos, thirst, and hunger. While being safety conscious, the Forest Kindergarten teacher needs to have a well-developed sense of trust that allows the children a chance to explore healthily without a sense of the teacher hovering over them. It is also important for the teacher to resist the urge to "teach" the children about the things they are experiencing as much as share in their joyful wonder of nature.

The parent-child playgroup leader naturally needs to be someone who loves adults as well as children and who has a high regard and respect for parents. In a similar fashion to how early childhood caregivers "teach" by being worthy of imitation, it is similar with the parent-child teacher. Of course, it is fine for the teacher to explain to adults how to do a handiwork project or something of that nature. When it comes to tending to and caring for the children, however, it is most effective to lead by example. A parent-child teacher may sometimes observe interactions between parents and their children that he or she feels could be improved with helpful advice. An important quality in the teacher is to refrain from judgment and try to accept all parents wherever they are on their parenting journey. Once a level of trust is reached, the parent will often ask the teacher for words of wisdom, and it is at this "teachable moment" that the advice will be best received.

The parent-child playgroup leader also needs to have pockets full of appropriate songs, games, and activities to share with the families. If he or she is a parent-infant group leader, he or she needs to be steeped in the understanding of infant development and have the grandmotherly quality of quietly guiding the parents in observation and exploration of the developmental stages of their little one. Having ready access to interesting articles to hand out to parents is also a good tool for a parent-child teacher.

From caregiver, cook, and director to preschool teacher and playgroup leader, we strive to develop a community of care, a new neighborhood in which children feel secure and loved.

Protection:
The Safety and Health
of Children in Relationship-
based Care

BY MARY O'CONNELL

Children must have opportunities to experiment, to find
solutions, to take risks, and even to fail at attempted tasks.
—Barry Brazelton and Stanley Greenspan,
The Irreducible Needs of Children

Safety

As I write this, the newspapers in Milwaukee are consumed with the tragic story of a young child who died after being left unattended for an entire hot summer day in a child care van. It seems every couple of months there is some story like this that scares parents, caregivers, and lawmakers alike. This morning's paper showcased editorials from folks who were, rightfully, horrified at the senseless death of a child. They called for reform...more rules, more systems to ensure the safety of our children in child care.

The fact is, there are already many rules in place to prevent such accidents in licensed child care. The Wisconsin licensing procedures for group child care are pages and pages long, and of the thousands of rules and regulations, most are regarding safety. I remember when, as a new director, I was looking

through the regulations with our licensing specialist and exclaimed about how many rules there were, and expressed concern that I would never get to know all of them well enough to make sure our center was in compliance. She looked over her reading glasses at me and said gravely, "Just remember, for every rule that's in this book, something happened to a child." Indeed, every accident that occurs somewhere in the state seems to prompt the implementation of another new rule. As a matter of fact, the latest incident of a child being left all day in a child care van prompted a new set of rules that all child care centers in Wisconsin are required to follow, whether or not the center provides transportation. And yet accidents continue to happen in child care. It seems no matter how hard we try to develop fail-proof systems, calamities such as this one still continue to happen in child care.

Stories such as this one shake me to my inner core and are a potent reminder that caring for other people's children is serious business. How do we reassure parents that their child is safe when they drop him or her off at LifeWays in the morning? Can we promise them that nothing bad will ever happen to their son or daughter while in our care? No, we really can't. But we also can't give in to the gripping fear that tends to accompany a "what if" mentality.

The Safety of Relationship-based Care

It was exactly this dilemma that I faced two years ago when I sat down to write a letter to our center's parents to reassure them in the wake of another child's death in a Milwaukee-area child care center not related to LifeWays. What could I say to these parents that would honor the trepidation they must feel about handing over their precious child to another adult each day, yet assure them that their little one is safe in our care? As I pondered what to write, I gazed out the window at the children and their caregivers playing outside. I watched as one caregiver had her group of children outside in the clearing, an area of the nature preserve that allows the children to run, climb on fallen tree trunks, and build forts with branches. There is no fence in this area; when a caregiver takes the children out to the clearing, extra vigilance is required. I watched as the children enjoyed varying degrees of freedom in their play. Since this caregiver had the same group of children in her care every day,

and had gotten to know them over a period of years, she knew which children could venture a little farther away and which ones had to be kept within arm's length. One toddler stayed close, playing near her caregiver, practicing her new walking skills on the challenging, uneven terrain. I noticed that sometimes she would begin to toddle too far away, and as though there were an invisible string between them, the caregiver would sense this even while she was helping another child with something and gently call the little one back. It was remarkable to watch this group of children freely explore and yet respect and understand the boundaries set by their caregiver. I then realized the truth about safety: The relationship between caregiver and child, developed over a period of months and years together, is what really kept the children safe. Of course we follow the licensing rules and have systems in place such as head counts and attendance logs, but what really provides a safety net for each child in our care is the fact that LifeWays provides relationship-based care.

As I drive through the city, I see signs for child care centers posted on vans and billboards promising a whole host of conveniences for the working parent. Twenty-four-hour child care, barber services, swimming lessons, and child pick-up and drop-off are among the list of promised services to entice parents to enroll their child. The reality is, the more conveniences we offer, the more adults we have taking part in the care of the child; therefore the weaker the relationship between adult and child, and the less control we have over the child's safety. For example, we have had a number of children enrolled over the years who have food allergies, some of them severe. The few times that we've had an incident of a child being served food to which he or she was allergic have always taken place when the child's regular caregiver is out for the day and there is a substitute. It is not that the substitute is careless or uninformed; it is that the child's food allergy is not living as strongly in that caregiver's consciousness as it is in the primary caregiver. This serves as a clear reminder that we need to keep the circle of adults who care for the child as small as reasonably possible to build and protect the relationships that keep the child safe and secure. When we are tempted to add services to increase enrollment, we must be careful not to put the convenience of the consumer ahead of the needs of the child.

Different Perspectives

Even in the context of relationship-based care, conflicts still arise around safety issues. Safety can be a "hot button" issue for those providing child care. Licensing specialists, caregivers, and parents all have different expectations, life experiences, and points of reference that shape the way they think about safety issues in a child care setting. It can be challenging to navigate through

all of these differences and determine the best practices for the children.

If you've had a chance to sit down and look through the licensing regulations for family or group child care in your state, you've probably noticed that safety is the priority. When a state licensing representative visits your program, she is hoping to find the safest environment possible for the children. The same is true for the fire inspector and other government representatives who may regularly inspect child care centers and home programs. Theirs is a world of *what ifs*, and the overriding theme of this world tends to be "minimize the risks by implementing and enforcing rules." It's important work and a very tough job, and you can imagine that if you focused all of your energy day in and day out on the enforcement of safety rules, you would probably prefer that children be wrapped in bubble wrap and not be allowed to take any risks at all! It's important for the child care provider to try to understand the perspective of the individuals who represent these regulatory agencies and to realize that we all have the same goal: quality child care.

As caregivers and nurturers, however, our focus is a bit different from that of the regulatory representatives. We know that for children to develop healthy and whole, they need to take reasonable risks. Children must be able to run, jump, and climb to develop body awareness, confidence, balance, and agility. They must be given the freedom outdoors in nature to try things that might be a stretch for them, that might cause them to trip, stumble, or become frustrated. Adventurous play that challenges and excites children helps instill critical life skills.

Increasingly, however, ours is becoming a society of generalized fear. The legal landscape of publicized litigation and our general fear level since 9/11 have created a culture in which we as adults have lost perspective on what is healthy, reasonable risk-taking for a child. Compared to children raised a generation or two ago, the children of today play outside less and have fewer opportunities for playtime that is not under the constant watchful eye of the parent, teacher, or coach. Parents are afraid to let their children enjoy the unsupervised outdoor play of their own childhood for fear a stranger will abduct them. When examined objectively, these fears are misplaced. About 115 children are kidnapped by strangers each year, according to federal statistics. Two hundred and fifty thousand children are injured each year in

auto accidents. In fact, the chances of a child being abducted by a stranger have decreased considerably over the past generation.

This generalized fear has paralyzed our ability to give children the freedom to take chances, make mistakes, and assume reasonable risks. Fear has become so pervasive that it has almost gone unrecognized. But experts in child development are beginning to take note of its effects. In the United States, the Alliance for Childhood has done much work recently to encourage parents to let their children play outdoors again. There is a growing discussion in the United Kingdom about the dangers of the phenomenon called "cotton wool parenting," and in the U.S. a new term has been coined: the "helicopter" parent—one who hovers constantly over his or her child. Play England, an agency that recently studied more than one thousand children and their parents, found that while 70 percent of parents said their own greatest childhood adventures were among rivers, trees, and woods, only 29 percent of today's children said their favorite play experiences were outdoors. Half of children ages seven to twelve have been forbidden to climb trees; 17 percent were not even allowed to play tag. Adrian Voce, director of Play England, said, "Constantly wrapping children in cotton wool can leave them ill-equipped to deal with stressful or challenging situations they might encounter later in life. It's not the end of the world if a child has an accident."

New South Wales Commissioner for Children and Young People Gillian Clavert shares that today's parents are so fanatical about keeping their children safe, the medical field is seeing a steep rise in anxiety disorders among the very young, along with an accompanying reduction in motor skills from fewer opportunities to play. "Over the past ten years, we have seen a real reduction in the range at which children can leave their family home and move freely. Research in state schools shows that children increasingly express fear of global threats such as war and terrorism, and have a general insecurity about their own future and their community's. These concerns mean they live life in a restrictive, guarded way, either as a result of restrictions imposed by others or themselves," says Clavert. Fearful children are likely to grow into fearful adults.

So, how do we as caregivers allow children to take the reasonable risks we know they need for their own healthy growth and development in this

climate of fear? First, we must try to understand the perspective of the other adults in relationship to the child. I've already talked about the need to "get into the shoes" of the licensing representative. We also have to understand that, for many parents, being good parents is synonymous with keeping their child as safe as possible. This is the message they have gotten from other parents, the media, and their pediatrician. When we understand where they are coming from, it becomes evident that first and foremost we must assure the parents that we take the care and safety of their child seriously. I'm not talking about a well-rehearsed sentence during the parent tour or a tagline at the bottom of the contract we've asked them to sign, but a real heart connection between caregiver and parent on behalf of the child. From this place of trust, we can begin a meaningful conversation with the parent about the child's need for play, reasonable risk, and adventure.

Next, we can share with the parent all of the safety measures we have in place to make sure that our trip into the woods or down to the river is well thought out. These measures include a cell phone and first aid kit for the caregiver, safety expectations for the children, and ready access to emergency phone numbers. Usually when parents feel we are taking the safety of their child seriously, they are thrilled and grateful for the opportunity for their child to connect with nature, gain independence, and increase self-confidence. When the occasional mishap does occur that results in a visible bruise or scratch, it is always best to call the child's parent during the day and tell him or her about it. It is much easier for parents upon pick-up if they have been given a little "heads-up" about an injury before seeing it.

Helpful Safety Tips

During a recent conversation in the LifeWays training, caregivers shared some things they do to ensure a safe environment in which children are free to explore:

Try not to put children in positions or situations that they can't get into and out of on their own. At LifeWays in Milwaukee we have a large boulder in the forest. Children are usually three years old before they are tall enough and strong enough to pull themselves up onto that boulder. Little ones try

and try again until they are completely frustrated because they want to join the big kids on that rock. They will beg any well-meaning adult in the vicinity to pick them up and put them onto the boulder. The LifeWays caregivers will offer words of encouragement and support, but we will not lift children onto the boulder; they must get onto the rock on their own. This may seem cruel to the outside observer. Why not just put them on the rock and make them happy? First of all, we've rarely, if ever, had a child tumble off the rock who climbed it on his own. Generally speaking, if he has the skills to get up, he can usually figure out a way to safely get down. A child who was simply placed there by an adult may not have the balance and agility to safely climb off and is more likely to fall. The same is true for tree climbing or other such skills. Secondly, this has turned into a true right of passage at our center, as little ones eagerly await the day they too will be big enough to climb the rock. Once they have done it, they sit upon that boulder beaming with confidence and self-satisfaction. Why would we rob a child of that experience?

Resist the urge to "rescue." There are certainly times when children need us to come to their rescue, when they are in imminent danger and we must act quickly. But often, adults come to children's aid too quickly or unnecessarily, and we can interfere with the child's learning process. There is value in allowing a child to experience frustration or to figure out how to get out of a tricky situation. When the child yells for help, the wise caregiver takes a moment to assess the situation. Often the child just needs the caregiver to be near and offer encouragement as the child herself works through the problem. If a child has climbed a tree and is afraid to come down, the adult can offer suggestions, if needed, as to where the child can put her foot, her hand, and so forth until she is safely down. When the adult simply reaches up and plucks the child from the tree, the child views the adult as someone who has magical powers to fix situations that she herself does not have. This does little to empower the child that she has the ability to solve her own problems.

Set boundaries and expectations for the children. When taking children out into an unfenced area, such as on a neighborhood walk or a hike in the forest, caregivers have shared a variety of ways in which they enlist the children's help in safeguarding themselves. Some tell the children that they must

stay where they can see their caregiver. Others will set boundaries that the children cannot stray beyond (for example, the big pine tree, the driveway). One important expectation of the children is that they respond to the caregiver when their names are called, and that they come when asked to. The children will need some reminders of the expectations, and sometimes there must be consequences for not meeting those expectations. But in general, children have an amazing capacity for helping to keep themselves safe when we show them we are confident they can do so. Of course, we do this in the same matter-of-fact way that we introduce any expectations for a child, without the overlay of our adult fears or concerns. It would not be appropriate to say "You must stay where I can see you or a stranger might come and take you away!" A simple "Harry, can you still see me?" will suffice.

Health

As with safety, health issues often present a challenge for caregivers who may bring a different perspective than other adults involved in the care of the young child. LifeWays recommends a holistic view of the care of the growing child, and this can often conflict with some current societal norms. We'll examine a few of these norms here, and explore how they can actually inhibit the healthy growth of the children.

Germ Warfare

We live in a society where the eradication of germs is highly valued. If you take a trip to a large supermarket or discount store, it is difficult to find any hand soap or cleaning product that is not touted as "antibacterial." Bottles of clear hand sanitizer are everywhere, on people's desks and in every mother's handbag. Parents can now buy children's dinnerware and pajamas that are embedded with antimicrobial agents. The marketing campaigns for air fresheners, mouthwash, laundry detergent, and dishwasher soap all aim to convince us that the key to our family's good health is our ability to kill germs.

This germ warfare is not only unnecessary, but can also be harmful. There is a great deal of evidence that the use of antibacterial soap causes more harm than good. The Alliance for Prudent Use of Antibiotics (APUA) states that

The Healing Basket

The healing basket contains the items found in a simple first aid kit, with the addition of some items to help soothe an injured child. It can be kept in a place where the oldest children can reach it, if needed, so you can send one of them to retrieve it when needed. The children love to be able to help when one of their young friends is hurt; it helps nurture feelings of competence and empathy. Some items to include in your healing basket:

- red (or other dark) washcloths used to wipe bloody scrapes, cut lips, etc. (White washcloths show blood easily, and this can frighten some children.)
- a pair of tweezers
- a thermometer
- salve containing calendula for scrapes
- gel containing arnica for bumps and bruises (don't use on open skin)
- aloe vera gel for burns (if you don't have an accessible aloe plant)
- Rescue Remedy (an herbal tincture to calm an overwrought child)
- Band-Aids
- small package of tissues for wiping tears and runny noses

soap and hot water are sufficient for most cleaning and hand-washing purposes, and recommends strong antibacterial cleaners only for hospitals and nursing homes, where patients are seriously ill or have low immunity. Why?

The antibiotics in these soaps kill more than disease-causing bacteria; they kill any other susceptible bacteria. Once the ecosystem is cleared of susceptible bacteria, resistant bacteria can multiply, resulting in drug-resistant "superbugs."

- lavender essential oil, for mixing with warm water for a calming face or hand washing, or for mixing with distilled water in a fine-spray bottle and misting the air

- magic dust

This last item is something Cynthia always had in her healing basket. She shares: "It looked liked a combination of very fine gold and silver glitter and was not used for physical ailments, but for behavior ailments! For example, one day all of the children were grouchy with one another, and there had been yelling and even some hitting. I quietly brought out the magic dust and very slowly walked around sprinkling an ever-so-slight amount over the top of each child, and finally a little over myself. Then I sat down on the floor silently. As the children gathered around, I slowly looked up, nodded my head, and smiled at each one. The mood was completely transformed, and healthy child play ensued. Note: This is most effective for children over three, but in a mixed-age group it is fine if the toddlers and twos get a little sprinkling if they want it. Also, when the children start to query about the dust, I say very little—perhaps something like 'It came from a land far, far away and is filled with good wishes and kind thoughts.'"

These items, along with an accessible ice pack and clean warm water and soap, should take care of most run-of-the-mill childhood accidents. Please be aware that in licensed child care, you may not be able to apply any gels or lotions to a child unless you have signed parental consent, so check your regulations before applying.

Some families we know at one of our LifeWays sites have struggled with a bacterial infection. It is purportedly one of those pesky drug-resistant supergerms we are warned can spread like wildfire and are impossible to get rid of. I did some research after it was confirmed that several of the children had this bacterial infection over a period of a few months, consulting both traditional medical sources and more holistic ones. My primary concern was whether our normal hand-washing procedures of soap and hot water were

sufficient to make sure this infection didn't spread. The results were clear, from both perspectives, that using antibacterial soap would only make the problem worse. Interestingly, the holistic sources also cautioned against a "panic mentality" surrounding the infections. Evidence suggests that bacteria can spread even more rapidly when there is fear surrounding their spread, as fear can significantly alter the body's ability to maintain good health. The staff took this advice to heart and adopted a much more relaxed attitude about the bacterial infection, encouraging parents to do the same. We are very careful with hand washing, but otherwise we have maintained the attitude that healthy children with strong immune systems, bolstered by organic foods and plenty of fresh air, have bodies that can heal themselves amazingly well. And you know what? They have. That bacterial infection seems to have left the building!

What about the child care cleaning agent of choice: chlorine bleach? Often when you enter a child care center, the smell of bleach can be overwhelming, as it is often used to wash toys, wipe down diaper-changing surfaces, clean off eating surfaces, rinse dishes, and more. Although chlorine bleach does not contain antibiotics, it is a toxic substance that can be harsh to children's lungs and skin. It can be difficult in licensed child care to avoid the use of chlorine bleach altogether. For example, the Wisconsin child care licensing rules require that the caregiver spray the diaper-changing surface with a chlorine bleach solution after each use. Often, several children are changed in succession, so children's bare, sensitive skin is being laid down on a surface that has just been sprayed with a fresh coat of toxic bleach. Not a pleasant thought, is it? There are several options of botanic disinfectant sprays that are clinically proven to be equally effective as bleach, but we were unable to get any of these approved for use in our centers as an alternative to chlorine bleach. After filling out countless forms and making many phone calls, I was ultimately told by our DCFS licensing agent that the agency did not feel they had the authority to grant us an exception to using chlorine bleach (which is odd, since their agency authored the licensing regulations.) Someday, we'll gather our forces and lobby our lawmakers to reconsider the wisdom of using bleach in our child care homes and centers when less toxic, equally effective cleaners are becoming widely available.

At LifeWays, we are careful to use bleach only when absolutely required to do so by the licensing regulations. All other usual cleaning activities, such as wiping dining tables, cleaning shelves, and washing floors and toys are accomplished with earth- and child-friendly cleaners. If we want to disinfect the infant toys, which are often in the babies' mouths, we just run them through the dishwasher cycle. Our overall use of chlorine bleach is minimal.

I fear that all of this talk about disinfectants is only distracting us from the most important point: *Germs are really okay.* A recent Italian study found that exposure to bacteria is essential for the development of an infant's immune system. The study showed that a baby must be exposed to germs during his first year in order to develop the antibodies needed to fight infection and live a healthy life. Perhaps this partly explains why, over the past fifty years as our germophobia has increased, people in developed countries have begun showing up in doctors' offices with allergies and autoimmune disorders in greater and greater numbers. Conditions such as juvenile diabetes, Crohn's disease, and multiple sclerosis have doubled and even tripled over the same time period. Almost half of people living in industrialized countries now suffer from allergies.

Amazingly, it turns out that people who have grown up on farms are much less likely to have these problems. Now, it's hard to pinpoint exactly why that is. It is likely that folks who live on farms are eating more fresh produce from the garden. They are also exposed to less air pollution. But scientists have also hypothesized that these people have immune systems that are better primed from the germs to which they have been exposed in their agricultural lifestyle, including bacteria from drinking raw cow's milk.

Illness

Won't children who are exposed to germs get sick? Of course. But it never ceases to amaze me, as I watch the children at LifeWays wrestle with each other, kiss and hug the babies, and huddle together under a blanket fort, that the licensing requirements are so strict about disinfecting surfaces and the amount of space required between sleeping cots. The children and caregivers share their germs pretty freely just in the course of their life together. And they do, in fact, get sick sometimes.

Michaela Glöckler, M.D., and Wolfgang Goebel, M.D., in *A Guide to Child Health*, share their insights and experiences from twenty years of practice in the children's section of the Herdecke Hospital in Germany, which is run along anthroposophical lines. Glöckler and Goebel give us a picture of the healthy human body:

> The healthy human being—standing upright, moving freely, with all the body's possibilities available—is a sovereign being and reveals the comprehensive developmental options and abilities of the human body. Illness, however, always imposes limitations on this perfection...each illness can be said to reflect a task that the body must perform as it struggles to approach the health of the divine image through its own efforts.

In other words, illness has a purpose in childhood. In purely physical terms, the body's immune system is strengthened as it comes through an illness, as is often evidenced after a child has a long bout with a virus or childhood disease. Often the child's parent will comment that after the illness, the child appears more robust and healthy than before the illness, many times reaching a new developmental milestone that was previously just out of reach. Beyond the purely physical level, Glöckler and Goebel's insights reveal that illness helps the child on an emotional and spiritual level as well.

> When the illness begins to pass, this means a victory for the child, a strengthening. The child has wrestled with the illness in the same way that it might have wrestled with a problem whilst learning something at school.

Given this perspective, we can see that as the adult treats the child's illness, our goal is to do what we can to help the child reap the benefits of the illness. *If the purpose of the illness is to lead the child toward health in body, soul, and spirit, then our task is to support this process.*

Supporting a child through illness is not something we do very well in our present-day culture. We are quite good at suppressing symptoms such as fever with Tylenol, drying up runny noses with Robitussin, and trying to speed up healing with antibiotics. Fever is a symptom with which we've become in-

creasingly uncomfortable. As soon as a parent discovers that a child has a fever, the pediatrician often tells the parent to use a fever suppressant to make the child more comfortable. My own experience with this is that within twenty minutes of taking the Tylenol, my previously lethargic child who was content to rest in bed was up running around, which seemed to be exactly what she *didn't* need to help her recover.

Glöckler and Goebel tell us that fever is a highly effective reaction of the body to combat illness and lay the foundation for sound health. Fever stimulates the activity of the immune system preventing the proliferation of viruses or bacteria. Research also indicates that fevers in early childhood prevent allergies. Predisposition to diseases such as eczema or asthma in infancy has been known to lessen after serious feverish illnesses. Beyond these benefits, fever also affects the child on a soul-spiritual level, deeply affecting the body's warmth organization and resulting in a healthier individual on many levels.

For these reasons, we encourage parents at LifeWays to allow their child time to progress through illnesses naturally. We ask that children be allowed to work through an illness at home, in their own beds, not merely as a means to avoid spreading their germs to the other children, but also to allow the children to return completely to good health. We ask parents not to bring a child back to the center until he has been fever-free for at least 24 hours without fever-suppressing medication. This indicates that he has passed through the acute phase of his illness. It can be challenging for working parents to take the necessary time off to allow their child time to convalesce. Once when my son was young, he had a virus that caused his fever to spike every afternoon and early evening for a full ten days. I was lucky enough to be a stay-at-home mother at the time, and I was able to support him through the entire illness, but there are many parents who don't have this luxury. As child care providers, we must encourage parents to build support networks for these times, relying on help from grandparents and friends, as well as flexibility from their employer. We can sympathize with the parent's need to get back to work while remaining firm in our insistence that sick children should be kept at home until they are well enough to return to child care.

Immunizations

Almost every country in the world recommends or requires vaccination of all children against certain childhood illnesses. In some countries, parents have no choice about whether or not their children will be immunized. We recently had a family enroll their daughter after having lived in several different European countries. Her mother was shocked to find out that parents in Wisconsin could sign a personal conviction waiver for any of the required immunizations, and thus not immunize their child. This parent felt that immunization should be considered a public health issue and all parents should be required to vaccinate their children. She felt that America's protection of the personal rights of the individual extend too far in the case of vaccinations.

This parent raised a valid point. Are parents who choose not to immunize their children simply relying on the fact that most other parents do? If so, they are weighing a chance of an adverse reaction to a vaccine against a very slim chance that their child will ever get that disease, just by virtue of the fact that most other parents assume a risk they are not personally willing to assume for their child. Is that fair?

But there are some other factors to be considered with immunizations. Many parents wonder about the ever-increasing number of combined vaccines, and whether these place excessive demands on the child's immune system. It's also difficult to either prove or disprove whether vaccinations change the immune system in ways that favor the development of allergies or autoimmune disorders. The most recent big debate has been over whether the preservative in immunizations plays a role in the extreme increase in autism in this country. Finally, the effectiveness of the vaccines is in question. Some people who have received an immunization for an illness end up contracting the illness later in life because the immunity did not last.

It's obvious that the issue of immunizations raises not only public health questions but also personal questions for parents. Wherever laws permit parents to choose which immunizations their children should receive, parents should be informed to decide whether and when their children should be vaccinated. *A Guide to Child Health*, as well as other sources, offers an in-depth look at each immunization, its side effects, its long-term immunity, and the effects of actually contracting the disease itself. One option many parents are

choosing is to wait until the child has reached certain developmental milestones (such as beginning to walk or speak) before giving the child certain immunizations. Another strong recommendation for parents who choose to immunize is to find a doctor who is willing to "unbundle" the serums, so the child is not receiving a cocktail of drugs, but can deal with one at a time. As child care providers, we must encourage parents to be as well informed as possible before making their immunization decisions. We also must make parents aware that if they choose not to immunize their child against whooping cough, for example, the public health department will require them to remove their child from child care if an outbreak does occur. In addition, we hope that parents understand that they must be able to provide their child with the necessary rest, treatment, and convalescence if the illness does occur. This can mean weeks at home for the child, and parents should strongly consider whether they are able to provide this level of care.

Lifestyle Choices

Do all of these choices really impact a child's overall health? A recent study of 6,600 children in Europe compared those children with relatively natural lifestyles (healthy diet, fewer vaccinations, limited use of antibiotics and fever-reducing medicines) to those with a more conventional lifestyle. The children with natural lifestyles had far fewer allergies and a much lower incidence of asthma. The choices that we, as parents and child care providers, make for our children have a big impact on their lifelong health. This is an area in which child care providers need to be informed as well as tolerant of individual parents' choices.

In our modern society, many conflicting views exist regarding the protection of children. We hope this chapter has given you food for thought as you seek to safeguard the safety and health of children, as well as a basis for understanding some of the choices and perspectives of parents and other adults.

Creating Your Community of Care

BY MARY O'CONNELL

I am a part of all that I have met.

—Alfred Lord Tennyson

WHILE MUCH OF THIS BOOK explains the how-to's of starting and running a LifeWays program, those of us who have done this work for a while know that the real magic of LifeWays happens once you start to build your community. It never ceases to amaze me when I visit different LifeWays home programs or centers how different each one is! Each program uniquely reflects the staff, parents, and children who belong to it; the way they come together to celebrate festivals; and the larger community in which it resides.

To give you a true picture of what a LifeWays community looks like, it would not be fair to give you just my impression, or just Cynthia's. To honor all of the wonderful LifeWays programs that have begun to spring up across the country, we wanted to share with you what some of the caregivers have to say about their own communities. So we asked them a series of questions, and would like to share some of the responses here.

Is LifeWays for Every Child?

Most of the LifeWays caregivers we asked gave a resounding "Yes!" to this question. As Margo Running, director of the LifeWays Childcare Society in

Vancouver, British Columbia, states, "A healthy home life is vital for every child's growth. The LifeWays model of conscious, caring adults who love the home tasks of cooking, gardening, cleaning, sewing, and supporting play are the best models for a child to imitate as he learns to move and grow in the world."

Most of the caregivers shared that the developmental appropriateness of the LifeWays principles made it possible for them to accommodate children they otherwise wouldn't be able to in a more structured program. Susan Silverio, of Spindlewood, a mixed-age kindergarten in Maine, said, "Working with the LifeWays principles and practices has created a nourishing community that has allowed us to enroll younger children (age three in the kindergarten of sixteen children) than we were able to enroll before."

However, most did say that the extraordinary needs of some children can be so great that a caregiver may need to make the decision not to care for that child. This largely depends upon the situation. For example, at The Orchard in Madison, Wisconsin, many of the children who are enrolled there have food allergies. The Orchard staff has worked hard to learn how to accommodate those allergies, most notably allergies to cow's milk, soy, wheat, and corn. Jackie Beecher, founder of The Orchard, shares, "The staff has come to see the extra food preparation and the opportunities for pedagogical work around food to be too important to miss." However, Ginger Georger, a home child care provider in Milwaukee, Wisconsin, who works alone, says, "A child who has allergies could be accommodated in a larger program with more staff, but when I tried it in my home it didn't work. My program is run alongside my home life in my house, with animals and two young adults residing there. I wasn't able to make it safe enough for someone who might be severely allergic to nuts or dairy or animals, because I'm not able to separate the areas used for family and child care.... They are the same."

Over the more than six years that LifeWays of Wisconsin has been operating its centers in the Milwaukee area, we have only twice had children enrolled whom we later decided we could no longer care for. Both of these times, it had to do with the child's specific behavioral challenges combined with our inability to work well with the child's parents. We have had many other children over the years who have had behavioral issues, but we were able to form

a close partnership with the children's parents to work through the challenges in a healthy way for all involved. This issue of parent communication was echoed by other caregivers. Jess Henry, director and lead teacher at The Orchard, said, "At best, the teachers working closely with an extraordinary-needs child's parents can work through situations in a way that actually benefits the other children who witness the process and the commitment. There have been a few times at The Orchard where I think the extraordinary-needs child took more resources or attention than was fair to the teachers and/or the other children. In these cases, we referred the child's parents to professionals better equipped to deal with certain behavioral and language issues. Knowing when to "call it" seems important to the overall quality of the program. Communication with the child's parents is *pivotal*."

Many caregivers, reflecting back, shared that determining whether or not they could meet the needs of a specific child in their program was a difficult and heart-wrenching decision. Susan Silverio describes it as an exercise in tempering one's own enthusiasm enough to admit your limitations. Margo Running shared that in her first child care program years ago, she asked a child's parents to take him out of her program due to behavioral challenges that made her fearful for the other children's safety. She shares, "I was young in my understanding of him, and I do wonder now what I would have done if I were faced with that decision today."

Most caregivers that do this work over a period of years begin to find ways in which to call upon the spiritual world for help with these children with special needs. Jess Henry shares, "Something extraordinary that we have encountered at The Orchard is that when we as teachers 'hold' a child in our thoughts and commune with that child's higher being (angel) through the use of adult conference, thoughts, and journaling, situations often mysteriously begin to resolve."

Is LifeWays for Every Parent?

LifeWays caregivers feel that for parents who understand and value the Life-Ways principles, there is an almost immediate resonance. Jess Henry of The Orchard shares, "Almost all of our parents value our homey approach and

gentle guidance. They see and appreciate the comfort level of their children who cry when they have to leave school and ask on Saturdays and Sundays if it is a school day yet. The children are completely comfortable at our program, as are the parents who like to hang around upon pick-up time." We have certainly experienced this at LifeWays Milwaukee, where we have had to set boundaries around the amount of time parents can actually linger at closing time, when caregivers are eager to close up the center and get home to their families!

Other parents don't seem to value or understand the approach. Susan Silverio describes, "There are parents who immediately resonate with LifeWays. There are others for whom it seems to be invisible. Perhaps they are looking for the 'program' that can occupy their overactive child. LifeWays seems to be like tuning into the FM station and finding classical music. While it soothes one person's soul, another may seek more 'stimulation.'"

Jess Henry said, "I believe LifeWays could be for every parent; however, we have had a couple of parents who didn't 'get it.' It seems to have to do with how their child is interacting with others and with expectations. At The Orchard, we tend to be more hands-off, allowing the children to resolve social situations and conflict naturally under our seemingly unnoticing eyes. In truth, we watch and listen carefully and adjust our activities, attentions, and groupings of children so as to assist them in their resolution. Parents have occasionally felt that the social issues should be more forced. In particular, we had a two-year-old who wasn't making best friends as her mother thought she should. We observed that this child was in much more of a parallel play level of development than the mother observed, and we were not worried that the child wasn't making friends. The mother did eventually remove the child from our center to keep her at home."

Margo Running believes that the key to helping parents become committed to the LifeWays concept is education. "Some families have surprised me, as they have stayed with us for three to four years. They fully intend to send their children to public school kindergarten where academic learning comes quickly, yet they are happy with their children being excited to join us each day and being happy and rested when they go home. Parents give us so much trust; there is so much information out there that says a child must be

learning and doing and producing. We give talks and distribute handouts about how the children are learning and doing, and that their producing is through movement and speech at this age."

Economics can often play a factor in whether parents feel they can put their child in a LifeWays program. Ginger Georger said, "If a parent calls and the first question they ask is 'How much is it?' the caller will usually not be interested in my program. Some parents just can't or don't want to spend money on early childhood programs. But when parents do see the benefits of LifeWays, they love it and tell other folks about it."

At our centers in the Milwaukee area, because of our small, mixed-age groupings, the tuition amount doesn't drop as drastically as children age as it does in programs where children are in much larger groups when they are three, four, or five years old. If parents haven't become fully committed to the LifeWays principles by the time their child is four years old, we are more likely to lose them to another program or to the public school's pre-K program.

Often what helps the parents feel a commitment to LifeWays is the community of care supporting their families. If they have been a part of the Life-Ways community for several years, have attended family festivals and parent evenings, and have become close to their child's caregiver, they often choose to commit, regardless of cost, to keep their child in that community until he is ready for full-time school. Oftentimes, when a family chooses a different program when their child is three or four years old, it is because we were unable to get those parents engaged in our community.

What Are Some of the Blessings of Creating a Community in Your Program for Children?

Years ago, community was created in our neighborhoods and in our extended families. Parents were supported in the task of raising their young ones by grandparents, aunts, uncles, and the other parents in the neighborhood. "It takes a village to raise a child" wasn't a political slogan...it was a way of life. Today, many parents are largely on their own when it comes to raising their children. Families are spread far and wide geographically, and no one is at home in many neighborhoods. Sometimes both parents need to work to pay

the bills, and even stay-at-home parents raising children in these isolating circumstances can feel as though they need support. LifeWays caregivers recognize the important role they play in families' lives and strive to help build a community of support for parents and children.

Margo Running shares, "Sometimes parents who are enrolling their child feel a bit guilty for needing child care. I tell these parents that only in the last generation or two have one or two parents been solely responsible for raising a child. Not long ago, there were relatives nearby or at least friendly neighborhoods where the children ran in and out of one another's homes. Before this, there were villages or tribes where everyone knew everyone and all helped to raise the children together. In these modern times, we have become so independent; we have separated ourselves from the support that was once taken for granted. What does a child need? Home life is important, but often we don't know our neighbors and must drive children to a scheduled activity in order to find a friend. How do we find community again? Child care is the beginning of reinventing of community.

"The child care environment is a community. Needs are met, words and emotions are listened to and find response. Parents may spend little time here, but get a sense in the morning and in the evening of being met in a caring manner with hellos and good-byes as well as 'How was your day?' They entrust their children to our community. Our work is to help bridge a connection between the child care community and their home life. The hope for the future is community—people being connected and appreciating and supporting each other."

Jess Henry shares, "Creating a community means working with parents to meet the needs of the children we all love and hold dear. It is wonderful to be able to tell the parents of the amazing and funny things their children do and say during the day. We both—parents and caregivers—love the children so. Seeing relationships develop between families is very rewarding." Ginger Georger shares that in her home program, parents have become a support network for one another. When Ginger needs to close her program due to illness or vacation, the parents call upon one another to care for the children. "And sometimes at the end of the day, I have an appointment after work, and the parents are all chatting in my living room as they pick up their chil-

dren. This is a wonderful thing; I love my parents, but when I've got to go, I simply excuse myself and leave them chatting!"

Watching friendships being formed between families is one of my favorite parts of my work at the LifeWays centers in Milwaukee. Recently we had two families move here from different parts of the world, both arriving in town with recommendations for LifeWays for their children, both knowing no one. It has been wonderful to watch these parents connect with one another, and watching their children form deep friendships at LifeWays. We have helped them find their community in this big city, and that makes me feel really good at the end of the day. As Susan Silverio puts it, "The quality of care that creates relationship also nourishes the caregiver." Indeed.

Community created in a LifeWays program reaps benefits for the larger community as well. When LifeWays children and their families go out into the world and share the blessings they've received from relationship-based care, the results are significant. What follows are the reflections of Nancy Price, a longtime teacher at Tamarack Waldorf School in Milwaukee, Wisconsin:

> In a large class of 29 first-grade students, I could see immediately that I had a solid group of children, leaders, who were interested in learning and who excelled in every subject. In my previous class, I had an occasional scattering of such children, but in this new class many students seemed to be not only eager to engage but also balanced and flexible, despite their various temperaments and personalities. They were cooperative, kind and forgiving, and helpful to others. Because of their ability to receive, digest, and transform the information I presented, we were able to cover an unusually broad range of skills during class time. The entire situation was quite extraordinary.
>
> Upon further inquiry, it came to my attention that most of the children in this core group had attended the LifeWays Early Childhood Center before entering kindergarten. But it was not only the children who were well educated prior to their arrival in first grade. I also found the parents of these students to be well versed in the philosophy behind our education, forming a trusting and supportive circle around the class and its teacher! I credit both our own school's kindergarten as well as the LifeWays program with helping parents to understand, early on, the importance of a healthy and whole foods

diet, low media exposure, creative play, and the healing qualities of time spent outdoors surrounded by nature. The LifeWays children and their families are indeed on an early road to a life of academic, emotional, physical, and social success.

Does Community Just Happen or Do You Work to Create It?

LifeWays caregivers all responded that community is something they continually strive to create. Susan Silverio shares, "A sense of community must first be a value and an intention on the part of the teachers/caregivers and administrator. Then a sense of community can be consciously cultivated in all aspects of life of the school/center. At Spindlewood, our board of trustees begins its meetings with a potluck supper. All look forward to this nourishing social time together. The family festivals are another important time for families to gather and to be enriched. Parent evenings are carefully planned to present a threefold experience on a topic by the teacher—an artistic activity and a time for sharing conversation and good food. Families can participate in cooperative orders placed through the school to obtain warm woolen garments and quality craft supplies at economical prices. As a support for all of this, the lead teacher takes an active interest in the parents, getting to know them in an interview prior to enrollment and making a home visit to each child before he or she arrives for the first day of school."

Jess Henry shares that at The Orchard they work continuously to build the sense and feeling of community. It begins with introducing parents to one another, especially new families. Then, new families are welcomed in the newsletter, and continuing families are encouraged to help them feel welcome. Caregivers warmly greet parents when they arrive and spend as much time as possible talking with them about their child's day. The caregivers invite Orchard families to join their own families on weekend outings to a pumpkin patch in the fall, and so on.

Ginger Georger says, "I do my best to connect people and have people together so they can build community. It takes time away from my own family time, but my family expects this from me....It's just who I am. I was outside working one morning with the children, and we happened to encounter

a woman named Ms. Sue, who also cares for children in her home. We both had seven children that day. My children were excitedly talking about the Friday night pizza party at Ms. Ginger's when Ms. Sue looked at me and said, 'I would never do that, have the parents over! When the children go home at the end of the day, I'm done!' I was left speechless. I am connected to my families, and I like it that way. This same caregiver mentioned a few months later that she had a huge misunderstanding with one of her child care families that resulted in the family calling Wisconsin state licensing to complain. I believe that forming a community around the care of the children is important. Trust and communication are keys to promoting healthy, happy family life at Life-Ways House and out in the broader community."

Marcy Andrews, LifeWays child care provider from New Mexico, shares this story of how a unique community is forming there:

One of the greatest teachers in my life was the midwife Elizabeth who helped me to deliver my son and later guided me on my path as a midwife. In a country where 1–2 percent of women give birth outside the hospital, she had somehow brought together a community where 30 percent were making that choice. Her midwifery practice was run out of a cozy little birth cottage where on any given day there were women of every race, ethnicity, education, and economic status sharing their experiences, learning from one another, getting a bit of respite from the world in this safe and sacred oasis. Elizabeth's accomplishments were astounding to me, yet she humbly would say that she had simply listened to and responded to a need that the community had expressed to her. She happened to have the passion to do that.

As I am writing this, I am in the process of watching a small community farm develop around me in much the same way that Elizabeth must have watched her birthing community grow around her.

I happened upon the passion when my neighbors and I were invited to harvest potatoes at a friend's farm in the mountains of New Mexico. We had already caught some sort of bug that was sending us out into the wilderness to collect berries, plums, apples, medicinal herbs, anything we could get our hands on. For several weeks we had found ourselves up late at night cleaning, processing, and preserv-

ing with an obsession that seemed to be meeting some primal instinct to feed our families. Meanwhile, our children's play had turned to harvesting, canning, and selling produce at the farmer's market. After our experience at the farm, trailing behind two donkeys searching in the dirt for precious nuggets of golden spuds, my son was waking up in the night asking "Where are the potatoes?" and crying to go back to the farm. I found myself in a dreamy state comparable to when you first fall in love, consumed with thoughts of growing our own food. I wasn't sure what had come over us. It was an inexplicable change coming from deep within that seemed to make little sense in the practical reality of our busy lives.

I am beginning to realize in that mysterious time, my ears were being opened to a community need that was being expressed through something much greater than myself. I am realizing this by watching how the community has responded to the mere uttering of the word that we made up for our project. *Kinderfarm*: a place where children can come to experience something real, something in the creative process, something palatable. The door was opened in those late nights of canning, dreaming, and wondering; and now the community has come flooding in, much faster than any one of us could have consciously worked to create. My playgroup is merging with the homeschooling community, thus widening the circle of children around us and creating something much more true to the feeling of family.

Our chickens laid their first eggs last week, and the children in my playgroup eagerly head out to the coop each day to search for the day's treasures. Our 1,200 onion seedlings that the children helped plant began sprouting today, and the children literally watched them burst out of the soil. Money has been deposited in the bank in the form of checks from CSA members willingly and knowingly taking a risk with us, enough to have our two-acre field plowed, buy our seeds, and set up an irrigation system.

When I really think about it, I would say this kind of community comes about consciously, but certainly it is a collective consciousness that calls it together. Because it comes from a place so much greater than any one of us, it takes on a life of its own and appears, then, to come about by pure grace. I imagine perhaps that the grueling work might come in sustaining it.

Are There Any Challenges to Creating and Sustaining Community?

When we opened our doors in the urban Riverwest neighborhood in Milwaukee, community just happened. It actually came barging in through our front doors! People in this neighborhood really value community and work consciously to build it at the park, in the little corner grocery stores and at the coffee shops. A child care center such as LifeWays that honors families' need for community was a welcome addition to the neighborhood. Parents are grateful for our parent/child playgroup, family gatherings, and open-door policy. Often in the morning, I'll find two parents chatting in the kitchen as they help themselves to a cup of organic, fair-trade coffee before work (at $1 a cup, it's a deal for them and a fund-raiser for us!).

But community doesn't always create itself so effortlessly. In our modern culture, sometimes parents are uncomfortable with this level of closeness and will back away. Some parents avoid family festivals or parent evenings because they won't know anyone there. They avert their gaze as they encounter other parents picking up children at the end of the day and utter a hurried and uncomfortable "Hello." We have definitely noticed this more in the suburbs, where people don't have as much opportunity to build community with their neighbors. It is sometimes a real challenge to find ways to engage these parents in our LifeWays community; but we know it's great for the children and their parents, so we keep trying! A new strategy for us is the creation of a LifeWays "blog" on the Internet. We're hoping this may be a way of creating community that will be a less threatening and more familiar way for modern parents to begin conversations that will eventually extend into more face-to-face involvement. As Margo Running shares, "Community happens when we look outside of ourselves and notice another. Some people have the knack of being present for another, and others have to work at it. This is where community becomes real: a place of support and nurturing, an extension of home, where we live and grow."

Several LifeWays caregivers, particularly ones who do their own billing and bookkeeping, shared that while community is a great thing, it can pose a challenge administratively. Jess Henry said, "A challenge I've encountered is keeping business matters (payments, tardy pick-ups, etc.) separate when you

get close to the families and have a tight community. There is occasionally an easy loss of business professionalism." Ginger Georger shares that she has found this challenging, too. "It can be hard to set boundaries in this community fold around money and policies. It is best to have your policy in place and make sure all the parents have a copy. When the time comes, stick to the policy!"

How Does Your Community Come Together to Celebrate Festivals?

Festivals are seasonal celebrations that bring the community together. Through the festivals, LifeWays centers and home programs strengthen relationships among the children, staff members, parents, and sometimes the broader community. Seasonal celebrations that lift us out of our ordinary day-to-day life and connect us with the rhythms of nature have been celebrated in homes of all cultures since ancient times. The planning and celebration of seasonal festivals nurture the sense of reverence that benefits the inner life of the soul. The gifts of the seasonal festival extend far beyond the actual celebration; there is joy in the anticipation, the preparation, the celebration itself, and the memories from year to year. An example of this that most people can relate to is the Christian festival of Christmas (before consumerism took hold of it!). Traditionally, the celebration of Christmas for families was much more than a one-day event. The Latin origin of the word *advent*, which is the time preceding the actual festival day of Christmas, means "coming," referring to the coming of Christ but also giving us a glimpse into this joy of anticipation. Preparations were made in the home—not the modern tradition of fast and furious shopping for gifts, but readying the home for the arrival of friends and family from afar. The celebration of Christmas itself included special foods to be eaten and family traditions to be shared, and the memories of this special day lived on in the hearts of all who experienced it.

In planning seasonal festivals, we try to honor the qualities of the season being celebrated. Festivals need not be elaborate to build community. Margo Running in Vancouver says, "We have family potlucks twice a year in spring and fall where we read a verse and speak a few words in honor of the

season." They also do small craft activities throughout the year with the children to celebrate seasonal changes, such as making an Advent wreath, felted eggs with little chicks inside, and lavender heart sachets.

Ginger Georger says, "I love getting parents together in my home program. My families have responded positively to potlucks and grill-outs. The children help me prepare the dinner, the house, and the yard for the party. The seasonal festivals are usually celebrated with stories and puppetry with just the children during our 'school day.'"

In my home program, I began to honor the seasons simply by decorating the mantel above our fireplace and sharing seasonal stories and songs with the children. The summer festival of Midsummer Day (around the time of the summer solstice) resonated with me, and it was the only larger festival celebration I held. Our family invited other families with young children to a lake and shared special foods, and I told a fairy story for the children. The children put out treats for the fairies, and the fairies responded by leaving the children surprises in return! We finished the celebration with a huge bonfire. Our Midsummer Day festival was a special event that our family looked forward to each year. To offer multiple festival celebrations each year would have overwhelmed me as a home child care provider. A festival should leave all those who participate refreshed and renewed, not burned out. Plan your seasonal celebrations simply and allow them to grow slowly and organically with your program.

If you would like some ideas for other festival celebrations, please read on. We'll explore how seasonal characteristics are honored in the traditional Waldorf school festival celebrations, and then how these festivals have been brought to life in an often simpler, more homelike manner in LifeWays programs. Susan Silverio shares, "In earlier years [while working as part of a Waldorf school], I held a festival study group and chaired the festival committee. Now, I aim to meet the essence of the festival in as simple a way as possible." Amen to that!

Autumn

In the fall (in the northern hemisphere), we focus on the qualities of courage, strength, and perseverance as we look ahead to the coming winter months.

Traditionally in Waldorf schools worldwide, the autumn festival is Michaelmas, the feast of Saint Michael, the archangel. It is celebrated with stories of knights and dragons, games of courage and skill, and sometimes community work in the school and surrounding grounds.

At our LifeWays centers in the Milwaukee area, we've found that the characteristic of courage resonates much more strongly with the older preschool children than with the very young ones, and we celebrate Michaelmas during our "school day" in preschool. During late September and early October, the preschool teacher tells the story of St. George and the dragon, and the children make a special dragon-shaped loaf of bread for the celebration. The dress-up basket includes the addition of shining armor for a knight, capes and crowns for princes and princesses, and a dragon hood. Also during this time there is the great work of harvesting the garden by all the children at Life-Ways, as we reap the benefits of our long season of planting, weeding, and watering. The children help the cook bring in the last bushels of tomatoes and other vegetables and are surrounded by the aroma of sauces bubbling on the stove day after day as she freezes our harvest for the coming winter months (alas, licensing rules don't allow canning).

At Susan Silverio's Spindlewood kindergarten in Maine, the children also hear stories about the brave knight and princess who overpower the dragon with the sword of light. Then, as a deed of courage during the Michaelmas season, the children make a hike one sunny October morning. They travel through the woods to a home where a local family invites them to gather the shiny horse chestnuts that are falling from the tree in front of their house. Each child brings back a bag of chestnuts that can be taken home and dried and stored in a basket for winter's play. These chestnuts are not edible, but provide hours of great fun being stirred into stews in the play kitchen, rolled across the floor, or packed into pouches as treasure. As a family festival, the Spindlewood parents, friends, and grandparents are invited to join the children one morning for their circle time, a harvest activity such as grain threshing or apple picking and cider pressing, a shared meal and a play.

The Orchard in Madison, Wisconsin, has found that since their program is small, it makes sense for them to celebrate festivals with the nearby Waldorf school. Their fall festival is a Halloween journey hosted by The Orchard. Vol-

Apple pressing at Spindlewood

unteers work long hours to set up paper bag luminaries along a short forest path that leads to different characters. These characters are nonthreatening, storybook people (the Baker, an apple fairy, Mother Earth, King Winter, a gnome, Red Riding Hood, etc.), who offer children a goody. The gnome gives a gold painted rock; the apple fairy, of course, gives an apple; Red Riding Hood, a cup of hot cider; and so forth. The children do not dress up themselves. There is a time for families to gather at the end, enjoying muffins and cider.

Spindlewood celebrates All Hallows' Eve and All Saints' Day (October 31 and November 1, respectively). After Halloween, the children are invited to bring photos of grandparents or other family members who have departed. The pictures are arranged in a place of honor, and the children hear a story about the value of keeping those we love present in our thoughts and hearts.

As autumn moves forward toward winter and the days begin to shorten,

we near Martinmas, or the feast of Saint Martin, celebrated in many Waldorf schools as a festival of lanterns. The emphasis of Martinmas is on the development of inner light through sharing and self-sacrifice, as Martin of Tours did when he shared his cloak with a beggar.

At LifeWays centers in Milwaukee, the children prepare for the lantern walk by creating their own lanterns. Each caregiver designs the lantern the children in her suite will use, and each one is lovely and unique. A small votive candle is attached to the inside of the lantern, so the child can safely carry it without risk of fire. The children's families are invited to join us on an evening early in November for the lantern walk, just as the center has closed for the day. This is a quiet festival (as quiet as you can be with up to seventy people!), so we dim the lights and illuminate the room with candle and lamplight. After the children have heard the story of Saint Martin, we begin singing our lantern songs that the children have been learning for weeks as the caregivers light the children's lanterns, and they go outside with their parents and follow the path through the forest. I have had the privilege to "bring up the rear" on occasion, and it is breathtaking to hear the singing and see all the little lanterns bobbing up and down along the forest path as the children walk along with their families. Upon our return to the building, we share a simple supper of soup and bread with apple cider. The Lantern Walk can be made even simpler by not including supper, as it is done at The Orchard and Spindlewood. The Orchard celebrates their lantern festival at a local park, a nice option if your grounds don't include a walking path.

At LifeWays, it is important to us that we honor the diverse backgrounds of the families that make up our center. One year, we had several families of Indian origin in our center, and with the help of the parents, our autumn season in the preschool included a celebration of Divali. Divali is the Hindu festival of light and colors, which is also celebrated around this same time with traditional Indian foods, songs, and stories.

Winter

As the sun reaches its lowest point in the sky, many cultures celebrate a festival of light with quiet hope and anticipation, including Hanukkah, Christmas, the winter solstice, and Kwanzaa, to name a few.

Some larger LifeWays programs have developed winter celebrations that are shared below, but these might seem elaborate and overwhelming to you. We include them so you are able to see all of the many ways this season can be celebrated. But please realize that a winter festival for families in a home setting can be as simple as inviting parents at noon on the last day before the winter break to watch a puppet show and enjoy cookies the children have baked.

Spindlewood begins its celebration of winter on the first Sunday in December with the Advent Spiral, a cherished festival in many Waldorf schools. The Advent Spiral is a simple and beautiful festival in a room lit by the glow of just one candle. The candle rests upon a stump placed in the center of a large spiral pathway edged with evergreen boughs, crystals, shells, and golden stars. A harp played by a grandmotherly neighbor sets a mood of peaceful anticipation. One by one, the kindergarten children journey to the center of the spiral carrying a hollowed-out apple that holds a candle. Each child lights his or her own candle and then places it on a golden star lining the path. (Younger children in LifeWays programs can walk the spiral with their parents, and an "angel" can be present to make sure the positioning of the candles is safe.) The celebration reminds us that at this darkest and coldest time of the year, our own inner lights serve to bring light and warmth to the world. The Orchard similarly celebrates the Advent Spiral with the nearby Waldorf school, and it is held in the school's multipurpose room.

At LifeWays in the Milwaukee area, the children begin the month of December with the story of Saint Nicholas in the form of a puppet play. They eagerly leave out their slippers on the eve of his feast day, December 6, and are awed when they find a piece of chocolate and a tangerine inside them the following morning. They spend the holiday season much as children would in the home, making gifts for people they love, baking cookies, and singing Christmas carols. We enlist the help of caregivers, parents, and children alike to create things for our Holiday Gift Shop, an event sponsored by the Quaker Meeting House that houses the Milwaukee LifeWays. We sell handcrafted items as a fund-raiser. Parents volunteer to work at our booth, and the preschool children create felt balls or watercolor notecards to be sold. It is a great collaborative event.

Spindlewood offers a grand festival, the Kinder Faire, held at a grange hall near the kindergarten in mid-December. The faire is part craft fair, part children's gift-making activities, and part family festival. It has become a true community event, involving creative handwork circles of parents who learn from one another to make crafts for the sale. Elders of the community are delighted to help children make gifts on the day of the faire. Midday, the teachers present a puppet play of *The Shoemaker and the Elves*. Then there is a knock on the door, and when a child answers it, Saint Nicholas enters and speaks of the coming of the Christ child, followed by his elf passing out a chocolate coin to each child. The board initiated the faire, and now there is a growing circle of people carrying it on. All of the proceeds benefit Spindlewood.

At Spindlewood, on the last day of school before winter vacation, from 8:30–9:30 AM, family members are invited into the kindergarten. According to the Swedish tradition, the oldest girl in the kindergarten dresses in white as Santa Lucia. She is accompanied by the Bakers and serves gingerbread to all of the families gathered. Prior to Christmas, the kindergarten's circle time is a shepherd play in which the children may dress for a part. The shepherd play then takes place at the Gingerbread Tea Party.

On the Sunday closest to January 6, the Feast of the Three Kings, LifeWays Lake Country offers a production of *Old Befana* put on by a local theater company. Like the Holiday Gift Shop at the center in Milwaukee, it is offered in collaboration with the church that houses the center. It is a lovely way to end the holiday season, introduce the children to a wonderful musical story, and open up the center to the community at large for tours and fellowship. It is a well-attended event, drawing many families from the nearby Waldorf school.

As the strength of the sun begins to return, Spindlewood has a Candlemas open house on the first Sunday of February where children may dip their own beeswax candles, sled, saw wood for candleholders, and enjoy a campfire with warm milk and honey. As Saint Valentine's Day approaches, the children at Spindlewood each sew a Valentine mailbox from their watercolor paintings. These are pasted on the wall of the mudroom, and children may bring simple homemade paper hearts for each of their classmates. The pre-

school children at LifeWays in Milwaukee practice their sewing skills as they create simple felt heart sachets filled with lavender flowers to give their mothers for Valentine's Day.

Spring

The festivals of spring celebrate the qualities of transformation and rebirth. As the earth seems to burst with new life, we try to honor this in our festival celebrations. In Waldorf schools, spring is often celebrated at a grand May Faire with musicians, maypole dancing, spring crafts, and games.

At LifeWays Lake Country, the preschool children mark the beginning of spring by traveling to the home of a nearby caregiver, where her husband helps the children tap maple trees for sap, boil it down to make syrup, and enjoy a delicious morning snack of pancakes and syrup. Another LifeWays family that lives on a farm brings in baby chicks they are raising for the children to play with and help care for. We begin planting seeds of all kinds for our summer vegetables and flowers. Mother's Day gifts are created with excitement. At Spindlewood, colored eggs, flowers, and stories of new life in nature delight the children. There is even a Father's Day Regatta, where children build boats and sail them downstream with their families. It is a busy time!

The families from The Orchard, along with those from the nearby Waldorf school, meet at a large park in the country for their May Fest. They enjoy a picnic potluck lunch

The Father's Day Regatta at Spindlewood

and dance around the maypole. The grade-schoolers dance and sing songs they've been working on for this event. The children roam in packs and play in the spring air. Some people play music, and families enjoy this as a time to connect. Spindlewood's May celebration happens one morning at the beginning of their school day, when families are invited to come from 8:30 to 10:30 to make May crowns and sing and dance around the maypole.

The LifeWays centers in Milwaukee celebrate spring with a family festival that begins on a Saturday morning in May with work in the play yard and garden. There is so much to do to ready the outdoor space for the season, and families are happy to pitch in spreading wood chips, hauling sand, building teepees for bean plants to climb as they grow, and digging up new garden beds. After a busy morning of working, singing, and good outdoor frolicking, we gather the children for a spring story and a potluck lunch. It is one of our most beloved family festivals, and you can often hear parents saying, "This is so much more fun than working in my own yard!"

Dancing around the maypole at Spindlewood

Summer

As summer approaches, on the last day of school at Spindlewood, a small bridge is set up in the schoolyard for a brief ceremony. Parents, friends, and family members are invited for an outdoor circle time. Then, as parents sing "White Coral Bells," the children are called one by one to cross over the bridge to summertime. Each child wears a golden crown and receives a flower with the words "May you always have love in your heart." Then an apple is given with the words "May you be nourished on your journey." Those children going on to first grade are dressed in gold silk capes and receive a crystal with the blessing "May you always be strong and true." The ceremony is followed by a trip to Lincolnville Beach and a potluck lunch.

At LifeWays Milwaukee, since we are a year-round program, we don't say good-bye to our school-aged children until August. Our summer festival is

held in the final weeks of summer after LifeWays closes one evening. The bridge the children play on all year in our play yard is brought to the clearing in the forest and transformed by flowers the parents have brought from their gardens. Only the children who are leaving LifeWays to go off to school take part in the bridging ceremony. It is an important rite of passage that the children eagerly anticipate, for it means they're growing up, and that the parents dread, for it makes them cry! As the children cross the bridge one by one to be bid farewell by their primary caregiver, the staff sings:

> *Something new is mounting, growing,*
> *Deep within me, outward surging,*
> *Seed is ripening, sap is flowing,*
> *Power streaming, light emerging.*
> *Go now, young friend, let love be your guide.*

Summer bridging ceremony at LifeWays Milwaukee

(Our caregiver, Jaimmie Stugard, wrote the tune that accompanies this beautiful Steiner verse.)

As each child crosses the bridge and reaches his caregiver, he receives a rose quartz crystal to symbolize love for his journey. A potluck supper follows, and it is usually our largest potluck of the year, as so many children bring parents, grandparents, and friends.

Last summer, at a park near LifeWays Milwaukee, we held our first annual LifeWays Reunion Picnic for all current and former LifeWays families. It was well attended, and people brought their own picnic lunches for their families, so all the LifeWays staff had to do was show up and enjoy seeing all of the children and their parents! It was a true community celebration to see so many families for whom LifeWays is a treasured part of their lives.

Birthdays

At the LifeWays centers in the Milwaukee area, a child's birthday celebration begins first thing in the morning, as the caregiver and children in her suite bake the birthday cake. It is a simple cake that is sweetened lightly with honey or maple syrup. Her caregiver has asked the child's parents a day or two before if they will bring in her favorite fruit to serve with the cake. Once the cake is mixed and in the oven, the children and caregiver cut up the fruit and whip the cream.

Later, as the children return from their outdoor playtime, they settle into the suite for a birthday story. Depending upon the age of the children, it might be told in the form of a simple puppet play, or they might all just relax and listen to their beloved caregiver tell the story of the birthday child's life. *Beyond the Rainbow Bridge*, by Barbara Patterson, has a nice simple version of a birthday story that you can adapt to fit your own needs. *Little Angel's Journey*, by Dzvinka Hayda, is a lovely picture book version of the story that works well for younger children who might not have the attention span for an orally told story. The birthday child's parents may visit for the story, or sometimes come just in time to join us for lunch and cake.

After the story, it is time to wash hands for lunch. The mood at the table is one of celebration! The older children are delighted that there are visitors

joining us for lunch and are eager to include the birthday child's parents in their conversation about the animals they saw while playing in the forest, their new rain boots, the new word the baby said today, and other exciting events. The youngest toddlers eye the visitors curiously as they intently eat their lunch. Eventually all are finished eating, and the caregiver disappears into the kitchen. Once the lights are dimmed, the room is filled with a loud "Shhhhh!" as the children wait for their caregiver to emerge from the kitchen with the cake, glowing with candles.

We all join in singing "Today is your birthday, happy birthday to you. Today is your birthday and we're happy, too," followed by a rousing chorus of *Happy Birthday*. After the candles are blown out and each piece of cake is served with a dollop of fresh cream and fruit, the caregiver presents the birthday child with a simple gift she has made. Perhaps it is a simple felted ball for a toddler, or a pouch with a polished stone inside for an older child.

One might think that in the age of theme parties and Chuck E. Cheese pizza parlor birthday bashes, such a simple celebration of a child's life would be considered boring. Quite the opposite is true....It is a gift cherished by the parents and the child.

We hope this chapter has given you plenty of ideas for building your own community. You will be richly blessed as you reap the benefits of growing a support system of families, and your children will thrive as they are nurtured in a larger community that shares similar values.

Regulatory Bodies and Professional Support

BY MARY O'CONNELL

Concerning all acts of initiative (and creation), there is one elementary truth the ignorance of which kills countless ideas and splendid plans: that the moment one definitely commits oneself, then providence moves too. A whole stream of events issues from the decision, raising in one's favor all manner of unforeseen incidents, meetings and material assistance, which no man could have dreamt would have come his way.

—William Hutchinson Murray

STARTING A CHILD CARE BUSINESS, either in your own home or in a center, can seem like a daunting project. What begins as a simple goal—wanting to offer loving, relationship-based care to children—can often get complicated very quickly with questions about legal issues, liability, and more. Many a child care provider has been scared away from offering child care on a professional basis because of these issues.

Hopefully, the information in this chapter will put those fears to rest. While there certainly are a lot of things to think about when you start a child care business, as long as you know what to expect, you should be able to navigate the process fairly easily. In this chapter, we'll explore the regulations and the professionals who are available to assist you along the way. Then, in the next chapter, we'll talk about how to set up your business.

State Licensing

The rules for child care vary by state in the U.S. The first thing you'll want to do if you are considering caring for other people's children is to contact the local office that oversees the licensing of child care. This may be the Department of Human Services (DHS) or the Department of Social Services (DSS), for example. In Wisconsin, it is the Department of Health and Family Services, specifically the Division of Children and Family Services (DCFS). You'll want to familiarize yourself with the rules pertaining to child care providers in your state. While it may be tempting to rely for information on the nice woman down the street who is unlicensed but takes care of a few neighborhood children, it is vital that you go straight to the source for the right information.

Most states have several categories of child care provider. Often, the various categories for each state can be found on the DCFS website. You can try searching at the county level first, then at the state level. Some states will allow you to care for children without a license but will put a limit on the number of children. In other states, it is illegal to care for other people's children without being licensed. There may be other stipulations, such as whether the children are related to you, their ages, and so forth.

For licensed care, most states differentiate between family child care providers (people who care for children in their own home) and child care centers, and there may be a category in between for large home child care programs. Once you have a good understanding of the types of child care structures that are allowed in your state, you can determine which one suits you best and order a copy of the regulations. Usually, it's available for a small fee from the agency, or you can download it from their website at no charge.

Caregivers often ask me why they should be licensed, even if none of their current child care families care if they are or not. It's really up to you, but keep in mind that your current situation could change. You may have a new neighbor move in next door who doesn't like listening to the children playing outdoors, and they'll decide to call DCFS to try to get your program shut down. If you are not operating within the law, you have no protection at all. Your child care would have to close at once, which would be very disruptive to the

children and their parents. As much as it seems to be a hassle to follow the steps to be legally licensed or certified, it's well worth not always having to look over your shoulder. There are other benefits to being licensed, including being eligible to participate in child care referral services, government-sponsored food programs, and tuition assistance programs for low-income families.

Each DCFS office has a system for helping new child care providers become licensed. Often there are classes you can take that explain the process, and many states require these classes in order to become licensed. In most areas, these classes can be found at local technical colleges or child care resource and referral agencies. Once you submit your application, you will be assigned a licensing specialist who will help make sure you understand and are in compliance with all of the regulations before your license is granted. The process can take anywhere from a few weeks to several months, depending on where you hope to set up your child care program, so plan ahead if you plan to open by a certain date.

Municipalities and Zoning

After you've determined what type of child care program you intend to open, your next step will be to contact the city, town, or village where you want to locate your business. You need to find out what types of restrictions there are for child care homes or centers, and what the process is for getting an occupancy permit, if you need one. It is helpful if you already have a building or site in mind, but even if you don't, you can get a general feel for what the requirements are.

Generally speaking, the larger the city, the more defined the requirements are for where you can put a child care home or center. For example, here in Milwaukee, the rules are very stringent about what type of child care can inhabit which type of building, in which kind of neighborhood. It can be frustrating to find a site that meets the requirements and then you may still have to go through a zoning appeal process. However, once you've identified a site that meets the requirements, the rest of the process to receive your occupancy permit is well organized and timely, due to the sheer number of these permits the city processes each year. In a smaller town or village, the re-

strictions are often much more lax in terms of where a child care program may be housed. But you may have a more difficult time getting through the process in a timely manner as you deal with a planning commissioner who only works one day a week, a volunteer town board that doesn't meet regularly, and so on. Usually, though, many municipalities try to make it as easy as possible for a child care provider to open a new program, because there is such a need for licensed child care programs in most areas of the country.

In a zoning appeal process, the owners of neighboring properties are often allowed to voice concerns about increased traffic, noise, and other effects of a child care program opening in their neighborhood. Many child care providers have discovered that getting to know the neighbors beforehand, allowing them to voice their concerns, and demonstrating your intent to be a good neighbor can eliminate surprising objections at your zoning appeal hearing. Introducing yourself and your program to your local alderman or other community representative is a good idea, as well. These folks are very invested in having quality child care programs in their neighborhoods, and can often help smooth things over with hesitant neighbors.

Your municipality will put you in contact with the building and fire inspectors who will need to inspect your space before you open. Besides the licensing requirements for a site, each state and/or smaller municipality has its own building code and fire safety code that must be followed. It is a good idea to get the inspectors involved early in the process, to make sure that there aren't any significant issues to be addressed with the building you intend to use. Sometimes these rules can be stricter in terms of sizes of windows and fire escape routes than the DCFS requirements, and these can be costly problems to fix. However, inspectors are often pretty good at finding loopholes, too. They don't want to turn away a quality child care program in their community if they can avoid it. It's always best to be as friendly and professional as possible when dealing with these folks.... You can never tell when you'll need them to be on your side.

It will greatly help your planning if you can try to coordinate the licensing process with the municipality process. DCFS will often require an occupancy permit or another type of communication from the municipality that states the town has signed off on your request before they will allow you to open

your child care business. If the child care program is in a building other than your home, you don't want to be paying rent for the space but still waiting for the necessary documents for weeks or months at a time. As soon as you've determined how long the process is supposed to take, double it! Everything always takes longer than you think when you're dealing with multiple agencies.

Professional Support

If all of this is beginning to sound a little bit overwhelming, take heart. There are people who can help you with the various tasks you need to complete.

LifeWays consultant. Early in the planning process, contact LifeWays North America and be referred to a consultant who can answer questions as they arise. Especially if you are opening a center, starting a LifeWays program can be quite different from opening another type of child care center, so it is worthwhile to speak with someone who has done it. A LifeWays consultant can do either phone or in-person consultation with you; he can make site visits as you get up and running; and he can even provide some initial training for your staff. The consultant can also offer suggestions of LifeWays programs to visit and observe. Eventually, you'll want the primary caregivers in your program to take the LifeWays training. For a current schedule of trainings offered, visit www.lifewaysnorthamerica.org.

Insurance provider. Every child care provider needs to have insurance. If you are opening a home child care program, call your insurance agent and ask what you need to add on to your current homeowner's policy to cover a home child care. Usually, what's required is just a rider to your policy that increases your liability insurance. Some child care providers have shared that they didn't feel this coverage was adequate, so they purchased additional insurance. If you'll be working alone in your home, you should be able to find insurance that meets your needs that isn't expensive. For liability insurance, several national companies offer policies for in-home child care providers. (You can try the American Federation of Daily Care Services: www.afds.com) If you rent your home, be sure to get your landlord's permission to care for other people's children, and look into renter's insurance to cover your belongings.

Once you decide to hire someone to work with you in your home program, or if you are opening a licensed child care center, you need more insurance than is described above. Your licensing representative will tell you the minimal amount of coverage that is required or recommended, but that may not be adequate to protect your business interests. Minimally, you'll need liability and property insurance. You'll have to have worker's compensation insurance if you have any employees. You will also require auto insurance, plus extra liability, if you'll be transporting children. Ask your insurance agent about errors and omissions coverage, which covers your business if a caregiver makes a mistake that causes harm. This coverage protects the business in a lawsuit. Lastly, if you are hiring anyone, you'll need to get insurance to cover illegal activity, such as child abuse or neglect. It's an unpleasant thought, but in the event of the worst-case scenario, you must protect the business, the children, and yourself. The other big area of insurance is health and medical insurance for the staff. Unfortunately, most small child care centers cannot afford to offer health insurance as a benefit, but your insurance agent can answer whatever questions you may have.

You certainly do not need to have all the types of insurance that are out there. A good agent, who has your best interests at heart, will write the policy so that you are adequately covered without going broke paying high insurance premiums. You can talk to other center directors or home child care providers to see what their coverage includes and how much it costs. There are also professional organizations for child care providers that can offer insurance information, such as NAEYC (National Association for the Education of Young Children), and local child care support organizations.

It's a very good idea to shop around for the best price on the coverage you need. Sometimes, the agent who has always insured your house and cars isn't the best choice to offer insurance on your business, because the company he or she represents may not specialize in the child care industry. You may be able to purchase the insurance from that company, but it will be much more costly than it would be with a company that fills that niche.

Small Business Administration (SBA). A small business consultant can help you get your business set up. We'll talk more about this in the next chapter,

but the SBA is an invaluable resource to anyone starting a small business. It provides workshops, courses, and literature to help you get started. A subgroup of the SBA is SCORE (Service Corps of Retired Executives). It has offices in most cities, and provides low-cost or no-cost consulting on an individual basis. The people who volunteer for SCORE have had successful careers themselves, often having started and operated their own businesses. They are happy to share their wealth of experience with new entrepreneurs. SCORE offices can usually be found at colleges and universities or in state offices. It is often possible to apply for startup loans and grants through the SBA, especially for women who are starting their own businesses. Ask your SBA advisor about any programs for which you may qualify.

Accountant. A certified public accountant is a necessity as you start your business. Choose one that is recommended to you by someone who is successfully doing what you want to do. An accountant will help you set up your business structure, register your business with the state, apply for an Employer Identification Number (EIN), and more. Your accountant can recommend a computer program or other system for business record keeping. If you are a home child care provider, have your accountant help you take advantage of all of the tax deductions available to people who run a business out of their home. It's important to keep good, clean financial records to utilize your accountant's time wisely. You want to be paying him for his financial and tax wisdom, not for organizing your records.

Even if you are a home child care provider, once you decide to hire an employee, you must withhold taxes from the employee's paycheck for the state and federal government. Your bookkeeper or accountant can set this up for you, or you can do it yourself by logging on to the IRS website. If you have an EIN assigned by the IRS, you'll use that. If not, you will use your Social Security number for withholding. The withheld taxes can be paid quarterly. Sometimes it's easier to hire someone to do your payroll. If you are hiring a bookkeeper to do record keeping, this person may be the one to do your payroll, or you can hire a payroll service. There are many online payroll services that take care of all of your withholding and reporting for reasonable fees.

Ask your accountant how to go about filing the reports that are due to the government monthly, quarterly, and annually. You may want to do your own bookkeeping, or you may want to hire someone to do it. This will probably be a different person than your accountant, who is more expensive to hire on an hourly basis than someone who does basic bookkeeping. You'll want to use your accountant for things such as answering financial and tax questions and preparing your annual tax return. For businesses, an annual return is required whether you are profit or nonprofit, and whether you have made or lost money.

Lawyer. You may or may not require the services of a lawyer. You'll definitely need one if you are purchasing a property for your child care business, to look over the contracts and represent your best interests. You might also want to have a lawyer look over a lease agreement. Since lawyers can be expensive, if you don't need someone for more than these basic services, perhaps you can find a lawyer in your community of prospective families who would do this work as a volunteer.

Business manager. Suppose none of this feels comfortable for you, and you just want to take care of children. You might want to consider hiring a part-time business manager. If negotiating with landlords, meeting with inspectors, establishing record-keeping systems, and going to zoning appeals hearings are not your thing, your first inclination may be to cut corners wherever you can and not do some of these things. This would be a terrible mistake, because all of these things are absolutely necessary to make sure your business is operating legally. A part-time person who believes in the mission of your project and enjoys taking care of all of these details is worth his or her weight in gold. When the very first LifeWays center was being developed, the first thing Cynthia did was hire a part-time business manager to assist with the initial setup. It was not a permanent position, but it made it possible to get everything started in good order.

As you embark on your journey to open your own child care business, remember that the regulatory agencies and licensing representatives want to make the process as easy as possible for every person who desires to open a

quality child care program. Consequently, there are many resources available online for everyone from the mother who wants to open her home to children to the person opening a larger center. One great resource for in-home child care providers is Redleaf Press, which offers a host of books, computer programs, and record-keeping systems for the family child care provider. In addition, become familiar with your child care licensing website as well as those of your local child care referral and support agencies to see how they can help you along the way. You can do it! In the next chapter, we'll help you begin to set up your business.

Business Questions

BY MARY O'CONNELL

Good fortune is what happens when opportunity meets with planning.

—Thomas Alva Edison

We will do all things in the material world in the light of the spirit, and so seek the light of the spirit that it may enkindle warmth for our practical deeds.

—Rudolf Steiner

ONCE YOU HAVE RESEARCHED the regulations where you live and decided to proceed with caring for other people's children, it's time to set up your business. As strange as it may sound, your child care business needs to be treated with the same care that you give to the children. Often people who are drawn to child care work do not feel an attraction to the care and cultivation of a business, but the growth and success of your child care business is important. It will be the support system for you, the families you serve, and any employees you someday choose to hire. You want this business to be strong and viable, and to stick around long enough to support all those who come to depend on it.

Jo-Ann Spence, longtime child care director, shares the following thoughts about caring for the business:

Once I realized that so many jobs and people depend on the school remaining open and solvent, it made lots of decisions easier. Many years ago, the economy was in a downturn and the school lost children. We had to lay off people and rent out our space. By understanding that the school must go on, I could see the BIG picture and work for better days. So, I see my job as working for the good of all to make the school as an institution strong, healthy, and caring. I think of the school as a separate entity with needs of its own.

In other words, a beautiful child care program with high ideals and the best intentions is only as good as the health of the business that supports it.

Unfortunately, we've seen too often the results of what can happen when someone has a great concept and starts a business, and the business fails within the first year or two. Many times this is a result of poor planning, inadequate funding, or improper systems. It is imperative that someone is caring for your child care business to make sure that these pitfalls are avoided. That person doesn't need to be you. But make sure that *someone* is in charge of tending the business end of your child care to make sure that you are one of the success stories.

For the Home Child Care Provider

As you read through this chapter, you'll find an in-depth look at all the questions one must ask before opening a child care center. You may be thinking, "But what about me? I just want to open my home to a few children. Do I need to know all of this?" Probably not.

Here's a checklist for the caregiver who plans to open a small home child care business. You will want to read through the information that follows in the chapter, however, to get more specific details about the following action items.

1. Go online and research the licensing requirements (see Chapter 8).

2. Take any required coursework, such as child development or CPR.

3. Get your own copy of the regulations and begin the application process.

4. Begin to make any changes you'll need to make in your home, such as building a fence, adding safety barriers, and so forth.

5. Determine if you will incorporate your business or have it be a sole proprietorship. More discussion follows on this.

6. Check with your insurance agent to make sure you are adequately insured (see Chapter 8).

7. Determine the ages of children you'll serve, your hours of operation, and your fees.

8. If you need startup money, where will you borrow it?

9. Start collecting natural toys from secondhand sources and/or making them yourself.

10. Use the LifeWays list of suggested equipment to help you consider what kinds of furniture, equipment, and supplies you will need.

11. Develop your forms and parent handbook (the CD offered at the back of this book can help).

12. Get the word out with flyers and online sources.

13. Plan a workday to have prospective parents help build the sandbox, put latches on drawers, and make other preparations.

14. Begin!

The Business Plan

Whenever you start a business, no matter how small, you need a plan. If you are planning to get a loan from a financial institution, you will most certainly need to show them a business plan. You may also need one to show a prospective landlord or a funding source. Even if none of these situations apply, you still need a business plan to make sure that you have asked yourself all of the necessary questions before starting your business.

People often feel apprehensive about writing a business plan, thinking of it as too overwhelming a task. To skip writing a business plan in favor of

just "winging it" and seeing what happens is a very foolish thing to do. Writing a business plan for a child care center is pretty simple and straightforward. It can be as simple as a ten-page document that answers crucial questions about how your business will be set up, why it is needed, and whom it will serve. Gathering the information for the business plan is the most tedious part, but your attention to those details will definitely pay off in the future stability of your business.

The Small Business Association's SCORE office (as introduced in Chapter 8) is a great resource for learning to write a simple business plan. The volunteers there can provide you with materials that take you through the process step-by-step. The CD offered at the back of this book includes a sample business plan for an actual child care center.

Here is an overview of some of the questions you will focus on in your business plan.

Business structure. If you are opening a home child care program, it will most likely be a for-profit sole proprietorship. There are benefits to running a business from your home, so make the most of those. For example, a portion of your rent or mortgage and a portion of your utility expenses are tax-deductible. You can also write off books, toys, and other things purchased for the home daycare even if your own children will benefit from them. If you are good about keeping receipts and maximizing your deductions, these can actually represent a sizable portion of your overall income. A good resource for record keeping in the home daycare to maximize your deductions is Redleaf Press.

If you are opening a larger program, you will want to incorporate it. The corporation acts as a separate person from the individuals running the business for all legal purposes, so the individuals are protected from being personally liable for the consequences of business activity. If the business should get into trouble financially, it's the corporation that is responsible and your personal assets cannot be touched. Some experts say that incorporating is also a good idea for the home child care provider who owns his or her home. Check with your accountant to determine the best business model for your particular situation.

When incorporating, you must decide whether it will be a for-profit or

nonprofit corporation. What's the difference? When you start a for-profit business, it is for the financial benefit of its owners and/or shareholders. A goal of the business is profit (although there can be other goals as well, such as high-quality care for children). The business pays taxes on its profit. A non-profit entity, as defined by the Small Business Association, has a mission that benefits "the greater good" of the community. Therefore it does not pay taxes, but it also cannot use its funds for anything other than the mission for which it was formed. Any "profits" must be reinvested in the organization.

There are certain advantages to being nonprofit. The biggest one is tax exemption. Child care centers and preschools can qualify for nonprofit 501(c)3, in which case the business does not owe federal or state income taxes, sales or use tax, although all individuals working for the business still owe taxes on their own income. Many nonprofits do not pay property taxes on real estate owned.

Another advantage is that nonprofit organizations are eligible for both private and government grants. People can make donations to your business, and those donations are tax-deductible to the extent that they don't receive goods or services for the donation. People usually feel more comfortable fund-raising for a nonprofit organization.

The nonprofit organization is not "owned" by its founders or its principal investors. It is overseen by a board of directors or trustees. This can be an asset when the board is active in helping to carry the responsibility for the financial and legal welfare of the organization and also is invested in the higher ideals and principles. On the other hand, it can be frustrating to give up control of how the business is run to a group of people who may not be putting in nearly as much time or interest as you are. If you do decide to have a nonprofit business, take care in choosing your board members.

Of course, we hope every person or group of people who start a child care business are doing so for the greater good. That doesn't necessarily mean a nonprofit status is always the right choice. It is easier, especially for the home child care provider, to incorporate as a for-profit entity. You can probably fill out the forms yourself, and the fees are relatively low compared to incorporating as a nonprofit.

One of the primary advantages if you run a for-profit business, either a

sole proprietorship or a limited-liability corporation, is that you have much more control over the operations of the business. Another advantage is the ability to sell the business. Should you decide someday that you no longer want to own this business, you could find someone who is willing to buy it. If it is in your home, you can sell the business without selling your home. The equity you have built up in the business and the reputation in the community are worth something to a prospective child care business owner. In contrast, a nonprofit business may not be sold; if the business closes or dissolves, all of its assets must be donated to another nonprofit.

A further advantage of being a for-profit business is, in a word, profit. When you are structured as a nonprofit, you'll get your agreed-upon salary and no more. There is a general legal doctrine that prohibits nonprofits from acting in a manner that results in "private inurement" to individuals (this means the nonprofit corporation cannot pay its employees higher than reasonable rates for their work). Of course, if you are charging market rates and paying the rest of your staff a living wage, large profits are pretty uncommon in the first place. Still it is wise to ask yourself this key question: If you're going to put a lot of time, money, and effort into this business, are you willing to have a set salary and no share of the profit?

All of these things are worth considering when deciding on your business structure.

Description of your business. First, develop your mission statement. The mission statement should be a clear and succinct representation of the organization's purpose for existence. Here is an example:

> LifeWays seeks to provide the best elements of care found within a healthy family, through relationship-based child care, preschool programs, and parent/child offerings. Our goal is to strengthen the relationships between parents, children, and caregivers by holding all in mutual respect.

Here's another example of a mission statement:

> Our program is designed to meet the special needs of infant, toddler, and preschool children in a safe and nurturing environment.

Our goal is to strengthen the bridge between your work and family life by creating a special place that supports them both.

Next, clearly define what will set you apart from others in the child care business. If you are opening a center with a LifeWays model, here is where you will focus on consistency of care, organic foods, outdoor play, professional caregivers, and homelike environment, to name a few.

Finally, give a brief description of how this business came to be. Is it a startup or an expansion of an existing business? Who are the principal people involved? What is the history of this project?

Licenses and permits. Please refer to Chapter 8 for a description of licenses and permits required to open your child care business. You will want to include a brief summary of these in your business plan.

Business location. Describe where your business will be located. Why have you chosen this location? What are the demographics of the neighborhood? Why is this neighborhood or community a good fit for your child care business?

Describe the building and the outdoor setting. Is the building adequate, or does it need renovations? How will you finance renovations? Is there adequate parking? Is there room to expand?

You've probably heard the old question: "What are the three most important things to consider when starting a business? Location, location, location!" While location may not be as big a factor for a child care center as, say, a convenience store that needs to be on a busy corner with lots of exposure, location is still a crucial factor. You want to locate your business in an area that is accessible to families looking for your type of care. If you have found the perfect setting with lots of natural space, a building with all the features you need, zoned for child care but it's located in the middle of nowhere, you might want to think again. While families might drive an extra ten minutes out of their way to get the type of care they want, most are not able to add much more than that onto their daily commute. In contrast, you might find a spot that's located in a populated urban area that is easily accessed by lots of families, but the area is so congested there is no natural play space for the children and there is a great deal of traffic causing air and noise pollu-

tion. While it is possible, it is more challenging to live out the LifeWays principles and practices in this type of setting. For example, you will need to find or create an appropriate outdoor play space and learn how to deal creatively with the higher level of noise. Finding the right location can take a long time, but it's worth taking your time to make the right decision.

Management. If you've decided your business will be a corporation, you will need to determine who will be on your board of directors. Check the laws in your state to find out how many board members you need to have, and how many officers. When searching for board members, try to find a mix of people who are passionate about your project and who bring different strengths to the board.

Whether or not you are incorporated, you'll want to answer the following questions: Who's going to be running this place? What are their qualifications? Do you need to find others to fill in the gaps where you or your colleagues are inexperienced? Donald Trump, the famous American entrepreneur, was once asked what was the key to success in business, and he answered, "Know what you don't know!" Most people are not experts in child development, finance, marketing, management, child care licensing, and community relations all at the same time, so it's important to be realistic about the strengths and weaknesses of yourself and your colleagues. When I first set out to open LifeWays in Milwaukee, I felt that I had a good understanding of the LifeWays principles and practices, as I had completed the LifeWays training and had been applying them in my home child care for several years. I had business and managerial experience, so these aspects of the business didn't scare me. But I had never worked in a licensed child care center, so I knew that one of my very first employees needed to be someone who had this experience. This caregiver proved to be a very valuable member of our staff those first few years as we learned to navigate the terrain of licensed child care.

Personnel. This is where you'll define the administrative structure of your organization. Will you have both an administrator and a director? What will their roles be? Who will they report to? Will you have different levels of care-

givers, and if so, what will they be? Who will the caregivers report to? What support personnel will you hire? Who will they report to? While LifeWays encourages collegial working relationships more so than a typical top-down business model, it is important for everyone to understand with whom the final decisions lie. In our LifeWays centers in Wisconsin, we have regular staff meetings and work closely together to carry the life of the centers. Care providers participate in considerations about hiring and firing, scheduling, and other things that support a healthy organism. At the end of the day, the director or the administrator carries the final responsibility for such decisions.

You will need to determine the wages for you and your staff. Try to network with child care directors to find out what caregivers are being paid in other high-quality centers. Paying your staff a living wage shows respect for the important work they do and ensures a more dedicated staff with a lower rate of turnover, which is essential for a program that is centered on consistency of care. What benefits will you offer your employees? Paid sick/vacation days, free or reduced tuition for their children, health insurance, and employer-paid training are all examples of benefits you might offer.

You will also need to determine the qualifications of your caregivers. What level of education do they need to have? Work experience required? What are your expectations for continuing education? Who will pay for continuing education?

Insurance. Please refer to Chapter 8 for a discussion of insurance needs. Once you determine the types and levels of insurance you will be purchasing, you'll include them in your business plan.

The market. Who is your "target market?" *Families with small children* is probably too broad a description of the customers you seek. Identifying your market is important, because you'll be inundated with more advertising and promotional opportunities than you'll have money for in your budget. You'll want to maximize your success by spending your time and money attracting the right people. Try to be specific about characteristics such as income level, lifestyle, education, values, and ideals of your target customer. If you want a

diverse population, both economically and culturally, bear this in mind also.

What types of advertising and public relations will you invest in? Advertising on TV or radio, or in large newspapers is not really an option for most child care businesses because of the expense. Once, when opening a new center, we ran a one-time ad in the community newspaper that cost almost $1,000, and we didn't get one call as a result of that ad. That was an expensive lesson! The best advertising for your business is, of course, word of mouth. Once you have a base of satisfied families, word of your well-run program will spread like wildfire. The tricky part is reaching those first customers. Remember to keep your target customer in mind, and try to find inexpensive ways to reach them.

Low-Cost Ways to Promote your Child Care Business

- Flyers. You can make them yourself on your computer and distribute them to exactly the households and businesses you desire.
- Welcome Wagon, or the like. Most communities have some type of service that contacts new residents. It is usually inexpensive to have them promote your program.
- Join the Chamber of Commerce. They offer many opportunities to promote your child care business, such as local fairs, holiday events, etc.
- The local Waldorf school or other like-minded schools. They often host conferences and fairs and may welcome a presentation on your program or promote it in the newsletter.
- Other like-minded home child care programs or centers, if they are full and willing to help promote your program.
- Neighborhood association newsletters. Quite inexpensive, and you can target specific neighborhoods easily.
- Other local publications that focus on your target customer. One of our best advertising vehicles has been the magazine put out by the local natural foods co-op.
- Make a brochure and keep some on hand at all times. A casual conversation with a mom at the park may lead to a new customer.

- Invest in a large, visible sign that you can put near the street to capture the attention of passersby.

- Host an open house.

- Make sure you contact the local paper about any open house, festival, or other event you offer. Sometimes they'll send out a photographer to cover the event.

Pricing structure. There are two ways to go about deciding what your rates will be, and you should use both. First, find out what the market rate is for premium-quality care in your area. If you are a home child care provider, ask other home child care providers how much they charge. Sometimes the local child care resource and referral agency will have this information. If not, you'll need to call around and ask. You'll probably find a wide range of pricing structures, because home child care providers often undervalue themselves. Remember that professional caregivers appropriately value the quality care they provide!

If you are opening a center, call around to the centers in your area that have a reputation for high-quality care. You want to align yourself with this elite group of child care programs, because a well-run LifeWays program certainly fits into this category.

Based on what you've learned about these programs and knowing what type of program you want to offer, decide how best to structure your tuition schedule. Will you offer five-day and part-time options? Full day and half day? Will there be a tuition discount for siblings? Will you participate in any tuition assistance programs offered by the county or state? Would you like to offer a sliding fee scale?

Secondly, with this tuition structure in mind, you'll begin to create your budget. Most of your expenses have already been covered earlier in your business plan, so you should begin to have a good idea of what things will cost. A sample budget is available on the CD offered at the back of this book. Once you have all of your expenses in your budget, you'll begin to compute how much income you'll need to generate to break even.

In a perfect world, the income you need to balance your budget equals the going rate for high-quality child care in your area. Of course, we don't live in a perfect world, do we? If it doesn't match, you'll start reworking your budget. Can you raise your tuition without pricing yourself out of the market? Are there other ways you can generate income, such as grant writing or fundraising for a nonprofit? Take another look at your expenses to see if you can reduce them without sacrificing program quality.

When setting fees, most child care providers make the mistake of setting prices too low, thinking that it will entice more people to enroll and that they can raise their rates later. While you'll likely have annual rate increases, it's very difficult to raise tuition much more than the usual standard-of-living increase. By then, you'll have families who've been with you for a while who are used to paying a certain amount for child care, and you won't want to lose them. *The time to get your pricing right is in the beginning.*

Financial data. Finally, at the end of your business plan, you'll make up a projected profit-and-loss statement and a monthly cash flow projection for the first year. These should be easy to generate from the budget that you created. Forms for these are available from the Small Business Administration and are also easily searched for online. The cash flow projection is particularly useful because it helps you project how much money is flowing in and out each month so you can anticipate the amount of cash you will need on hand to fund your growing business.

Funding

Once you have your business plan, you should begin to have an idea of how much money you'll need to start this business, and how much additional money you'll need to keep it going until the business is generating enough income to support itself. One of the primary causes of failure of a new business is inadequate cash on hand to support its growth.

If this is your own business, you will fund the new business venture. If you need to, you can borrow money to fund your initial expenses. You can take your business plan to your bank or other people you know who may be interested in investing. The Small Business Association offers seminars on

how to obtain low-interest loans for small businesses. There are often special loan opportunities available for women entrepreneurs.

If you are starting a corporation, the board will need to determine how funding will be obtained. It may be a bit more difficult to get a bank loan because the bank usually wants someone to guarantee the loan with his or her assets, and the whole idea behind incorporating is the protection of the individuals' assets. Individual investors may be a better source for loans in this case. You might approach the families who want you to care for their children and ask them for a low- or no-interest loan to help get the business going. You can also charge families an upfront materials fee or deposit that will help to fund some, but not all, of your startup costs. Finally, there might be an influential local person who feels strongly about having this program in the community and is willing to loan some money.

For a nonprofit corporation, you can solicit tax-deductible donations from people who want to support your program. You can apply for grants as well. Another option is to host a large fund-raising event to raise money for the new child care program.

Systems

Developing the proper systems for everything from billing and debt collection, to expectations of parents, to evaluation of staff members can seem a little overwhelming. You may come up with a system for something only to find, a month later, that it doesn't make sense to do it that way. There may be things for which you never thought you needed a system but you quickly realize that you've got to standardize the way you are handling them. Systems can certainly change as you go along. But the most important thing is to think them through in the first place because it ensures that everyone is treated fairly and understands what is expected.

Payment systems. Especially for the home child care provider, collecting payments can be difficult. It is hard to ask parents for money at the end of the day as you are sharing heartwarming stories about their child. Wearing both hats—administrator and caregiver—can be a real challenge. By having regular systems of billing and collecting money, you can eliminate some, but not

all, of the uncomfortable moments. Make sure your policies are in writing and in parents' hands before they start in your program.

When making your policies, here are a few things to consider: Will you charge a registration fee? A deposit? Will parents be expected to pay weekly, biweekly, or monthly? What happens if parents don't pay on time? Is there a late-payment fee? What if their child is sick or they decide not to bring him or her? Do they still have to pay? What if you are unavailable to care for children because you (or one of your own children) are ill? Will you be closed for holidays or vacations? Will you charge for days you are closed? Once you have answered all of these questions, you'll design a contract for parents to sign that clearly states what they are agreeing to and under what circumstances the contract can be terminated. A sample LifeWays Registration Contract is available on the CD offered at the back of this book.

Even when you've got good systems in place for collecting payments, you will have parents who do not follow them. Often, people just need a reminder of the expectations. Sometimes, people have situations that prevent them from paying on time. You will need to decide how you are going to handle parents who can't pay their bills. If you are a generous person, you may be tempted to let an unpaid balance go for a while, hoping the parent will catch up later. Realistically, a parent who is having a difficult time coming up with $500 this month is not likely to have an easier time coming up with $1,000 next month. If people get too far behind in their payments, most likely they will end up leaving your program because they can't pay. You will be out hundreds of dollars, and their child has to deal with the stress of losing a beloved caregiver. You're not doing anyone any favors by overlooking a late-payment situation. Every child care provider probably has a story to share in which she learned this lesson. In general, if you can get a parent to discuss and commit to a payment plan with you, you have a greater chance of success than if you just take a "wait and see" approach. If you can afford to do so, it is better to renegotiate a payment plan that the family can actually do rather than allow them to continue to say *the check's in the mail* when they truly cannot pay that amount. You can also encourage them to apply for whatever support systems might be available to them at their income level or reach out to family and friends who have the best interest of their child(ren) at heart.

Parent handbook. In your parent handbook, you'll introduce all of the policies that affect parents, such as how to enroll a child, payment policies, attendance and scheduling, and what the parent needs to provide. You'll also want to talk about how enrollment is terminated (either by you or by the parent) and the procedure that goes along with that.

You will talk about your child development philosophy and how you handle discipline, parent communication, emergency procedures, health care policies, and nutrition, to name a few of the topics. If you are going to be licensed, the licensing agency will likely tell you what needs to be covered in your parent handbook. For a home child care provider, the parent handbook may be only a few pages long. For a child care center, it may be up to twenty-five pages long. Try not to let it get too long or parents won't read it. A sample parent handbook for a home child care and a child care center are included in the CD offered at the back of this book.

Operating policies and procedures. If you are a home child care provider working alone, you probably don't need to put your policies and procedures in writing unless it is required by licensing. Once you begin to hire employees, it is important to have a written document that outlines your policies. For licensed centers, the licensing agency usually has a format to follow to make sure everything is covered. Your policies and procedures will cover everything you discussed in your parent handbook, as well as specifics about things such as admission procedures, child guidance, continuing education, curriculum and programming, diapering procedures, hand-washing and first aid procedures, food preparation procedures, administrative structure, personnel policies, and grievance procedures.

When you hire new employees, you should sit down with them and read through the policies and procedures. Make sure they understand that they are expected to follow these. Follow up with them if you see that they are not following the policies and procedures, because it is a lot to take in at first. I've had caregivers who have worked for LifeWays for several years and I'll notice one day that they aren't following our procedures. Oftentimes, when I bring it up, they share that they just started doing something a different way and never realized it. For this reason, it's important to revisit the policies

and procedures every once in a while to see if you are still doing what you said you were going to do. If not, you need to refocus and get back to the policies and procedures or ask yourself if the policies and procedures need to be rewritten to reflect a more accurate picture of what's really happening.

Staff evaluation. If you are a home child care provider working alone, you obviously don't need a formal evaluation process, but you will want to set aside some quiet time on at least an annual basis to look through the Life-Ways principles and practices and objectively examine where you would like to improve in the coming year. Perhaps you know of someone who is doing similar work who can be your support partner in setting goals for the coming year and helping you meet them. For example, maybe after reflecting on the LifeWays principles and practices, you determine that you'd like to incorporate more of the nurturing arts (hair brushing, footbaths, lap games and stories, etc.). Your support partner can help you develop a plan of how to make sure it happens and then check in with you monthly to see how it's going. You can do the same for him or her.

Once you hire someone, either in a home or center setting, you'll need to develop a system to evaluate the performance of that person. This is necessary not only to maintain the quality of your program, but also to develop your staff and provide a format for at least an annual conversation to reflect and set goals together. It can also be linked to an annual pay increase.

Sample evaluation forms are provided in the CD offered at the back of this book.

You will need to determine how the evaluation process will take place and make sure it is consistent with each member of the staff. The process should be clearly communicated ahead of time so people know what to expect. The form you'll use, if any, should be distributed to each member of the staff so there are no surprises about job expectations. You want to avoid sitting down with a staff member for an evaluation meeting only to hear him say, "I didn't know I was supposed to be doing that!"

Here are a few questions you should answer before entering an evaluation process: Will people do a self-evaluation before they sit down with you for your conversation? Will you complete a separate evaluation of them based

on your observations? Will you ask staff members for input on others' evaluations? If there are areas of improvement needed, how will you follow up on these? How will you follow up to ensure goals that are set during the performance review are being met? Will you tie pay increases to performance evaluations? If so, how will you go about determining the pay increase amount, and is it objective and fair to all?

Of course, beyond the annual performance review, there should be daily evaluation and feedback. The director, as well as the rest of the staff, should always be in conversation about things that have been observed that need to be improved, and things that are being done well. Creating a culture that allows for this conversation is important. While many of us don't like conflict, we must find a way to bring up issues that need to be resolved long before the annual performance review. It is not fair to say nothing to a staff member about an area that needs significant improvement, only to spring it on her or him at the annual performance review.

While much of what you have just read may seem somewhat unappealing or not representative of the reason you want to be involved with child care, let's return to the thought at the beginning of this chapter: Your child care business needs to be treated with the same care that you give to the children. You can think of creating budgets, business plans, policies, and procedures as providing good nutrition, healthy rhythms, and creative care to the business infrastructure that indeed will support the nutrition, rhythms, and care of the families and caregivers who matter to you the most. Another line in the Steiner verse quoted at the beginning of this chapter states, *"Seek real, practical material life, but seek in such a way that the spirit which dwells within is not deadened for you."* The more you can enter into these foundational processes with interest, the more alive they can become for you.

Once you have addressed all the areas mentioned in this chapter, you are ready to open your child care business! Your business has a far better chance of success because of your preparedness, and you can rest assured that many children and their families will benefit from your home away from home because you took the time to ensure a healthy business to support it. Good luck to you, and please let us know how LifeWays North America can support you in your work!

10

Supporting You in Your Work— LifeWays North America

BY CYNTHIA ALDINGER

Tell me and I will forget
Show me and I will remember
Involve me and I will understand

—Confucius

The master in the art of living makes little distinction between his work and his play, his labor and his leisure, his mind and his body, his information and his recreation, his love and his religion. He hardly knows which is which. He simply pursues his vision of excellence at whatever he does, leaving others to decide whether he is working or playing. To him he's always doing both.

—Zen Buddhism

History

In order to give a brief overview of the development of LifeWays North America, it seems appropriate to acknowledge the educational impulse out of which our work has sprung. Waldorf education (or Steiner education as it is known in other parts of the world) will soon celebrate the one-hundredth anniver-

sary of the first Waldorf school, founded in 1919 in Stuttgart, Germany. While various curricular ideals and subjects were developed for elementary and high school, no curriculum was suggested for early childhood. Rather, Rudolf Steiner gave numerous lectures on child development that included deep insight regarding the child from birth to seven. Consider this statement from Dr. Steiner found in the book *The Child's Changing Consciousness*:

> The task of the kindergarten teacher is to adapt the practical activities of daily life so that they are suitable for the child's imitation through play. . . . The activities of children in kindergarten must be derived directly from life itself rather than being "thought out" by the intellectualized culture of adults. In the kindergarten, the most important thing is to give the children the opportunity to directly imitate life itself.

Eventually kindergartens were created, and they continue to be some of the most creative, play-oriented, nature-based, and child-friendly kindergartens in the world. It was through the privilege of being a Waldorf kindergarten teacher that the door was opened for me to establish the foundations of LifeWays North America.

While attending an international Waldorf kindergarten conference in Great Britain in 1995, I was approached by my friend Brian Swain, a successful business consultant, with this question: "What are you going to do about child care?" He and several of his colleagues had been discussing their perception that the current approach to child care was not really preparing children for practical, daily life or supporting them in developmentally appropriate ways. While his question came as a surprise, it also came at a providential time. During that conference, I encountered the inspiring work of Helle Heckman, a Danish Waldorf child care pioneer. Having been a Waldorf kindergarten teacher for several years, it was intriguing to think of having children for longer than just the morning program, allowing an expanded flow of the day with more time outside, a family-style meal in the middle of the day, and a good sleep after lunch.

It was a few months after the conference in England that I first wrote down a vision for Steiner-inspired child care that would be based on the routine activities and natural rhythms of healthy home life, bathed in the

warmth of secure relationships and family-style mixed ages, and made to feel as noninstitutional as possible. This first written vision evolved over time into the current Principles and Practices of LifeWays Childcare. A few years after writing these, I experienced the work of Bernadette Raichle in New Zealand, whose early childhood center, Awhina, filled me with wonder and delight. While bringing new inspiration and ideas to our LifeWays work, observing at Awhina provided affirmation of how homelike, simple living serves all the fundamental needs of young children and their caregivers.

When my friend and colleague Rena Osmer and I came up with the name *LifeWays* to represent the nature of the care we were hoping to develop, we contacted our colleagues Gudrun Davy, Bons Voors, Patti Smith, and Signe Schaefer (editors of two Lifeways books) and Lee Sturgeon Day, who uses the name in her biography and counseling work. With their blessings in place, and with the organizing support of Lori Barian and other Wisconsin friends, the first LifeWays center was opened in Wisconsin in September 1998. It was the pilot child care project for children three months to six years old and hosted the first LifeWays training.

Over time, we added suggested practices for parent-child and parent-infant programs, mostly inspired by our Waldorf colleagues doing that work. And in recent years, we have come to realize how our trainings also support the growth and development of parents seeking a deeper understanding of child development and homemaking.

Through the sponsorship of the Waldorf Early Childhood Association of North America, several organizations—including Rudolf Steiner Foundation, Pritzker Cousins Foundation, Michael Foundation, and private entrepreneurs—offered grant support for the early development of LifeWays. By 1999, LifeWays of Wisconsin was its own nonprofit corporation. It continues today as the organization fostering the development of LifeWays centers in Wisconsin, directed by Mary O'Connell.

Our national organization, LifeWays North America, formed a few years later after a group of individuals began meeting on a regular basis at Rudolf Steiner College in California. LifeWays North America has become a multi-service organization providing consulting and training for family child care providers, child care centers, parent-child teachers, home-based preschool

teachers, after-school care providers, and parents. There are several Life-Ways child care centers, home child care programs, and parent-child programs throughout North America. Some are in close association with local Waldorf schools and others are not involved with Waldorf communities. Life-Ways trainings are also available now in several locations. More information is available at www.lifewaysnorthamerica.org.

LifeWays Training

Before describing our LifeWays trainings, I must admit that children and families in airports are my textbooks these days. They teach me about flexibility, frailty, frazzledness, and fun. Typically the first and last have to do with the children, and the middle ones have to do with the parents! However, I have observed my share of frazzled little ones, the contagion of which infects the parents. I do my best to bring a little relief when I can, engaging the child in a game of peek-a-boo, for instance, while a tired mother or father recovers. I did not come up with this idea. I learned it from a toddler in a St. Louis airport. While waiting to board, an announcement came that our flight would be delayed—again—and the sense of frustration among the adults began to create a heavy mood. Meetings and deadlines were going to be missed, reunions with loved ones delayed, and business deals put at risk! A toddler who had been sleeping peacefully in mother's arms began to stir. As he slid down from her lap, he began to walk around the rows of bolted-down seats, occasionally dipping his little head behind a chair and then quickly peeking out at whomever he could engage with his twinkling eyes. Smiles began to emerge on faces, shoulders began to relax, and a soft chuckle began to float in the air. A sense of balance returned, and we all remembered that life goes on. I have experienced a number of similar incidents.

Children are like heart medicine. *Of course, there are other aspects to caring for children!* But beyond the exhaustion, the worry, the fears, and the fuss, they lift our spirits and give us hope. They come into the world, one could say, with the expectation that the world is good and right, and whatever they encounter, they encounter with this expectation. Only through overt teachings or unfortunate experiences will a young child potentially develop

distrust or fear. Left to their own inner urges and open gesture, children want to experience through their senses everything they meet. The world is full of wonder for them.

How is it that these fresh doses of optimism enter the world every time a child is born? Where have they been before arriving here—on vacation? Freed from the weight of worldly concerns, held in the arms of the angels, and fresh from a cosmic journey too profound to describe here, they show up at our homes or in our hospital rooms as amazing spiritual beings wrapped up in tiny packages called infants.

If one word were to be emblazoned across the forehead of a newborn, I think it would be *Yes!*—a new life, a new family, a new world of experience to taste, touch, smell, breathe, hear, see, do, and be. You can tell by looking at them, especially when they are falling asleep, that they are still as much a part of heaven as they are of the earth.

They spend the first year changing from horizontal to vertical, from an armful of wiggling warmth and softness to a tiny tower of stumbling, tumbling collapsible energy. *Up* and *down* comprise whole worlds of experience. While conquering gravity, they also shift from universal babbling to one-word sentences and spend the following year collecting a vocabulary that eventually brings them into the community of fellow conversant beings. By age three, they have typically moved from the verbal village of *Me-Mine-No* over the bridge of the incessant *Why?* and toward the wonderful world of *Look at Me!* Staking their personal claim of individuality, no longer totally wrapped up in identifying themselves as extensions of Mommy and Daddy, they begin living parallel lives—sometimes in the mundane every day of helping with simple chores any four-year-old could handle and sharing belly laughs over uproariously funny bodily functions, and sometimes in the creative and inviting world of make-believe that is the fundamental right of every young child to inhabit. This dual capacity increases as the child grows toward five and six. Standing on the threshold between early childhood and middle childhood, we often encounter an independence that is accompanied by such endearing phrases as *You're not the boss of me!*

This roller coaster of human expression takes us through early childhood. The adventure continues as we travel through middle childhood, adolescence,

and the threshold of adulthood with our children. Most of us had no idea when we purchased our one-way ticket to parenthood that we were in for the ride of our lives. Whether we are parenting our own children or caring for other people's children, it is the ultimate magical mystery tour!

LifeWays training is a tour bus that we can climb aboard together to explore child development, our own development, practical and artistic life skills, the tools of the trade for creating child care settings or parent-child programs, and an introductory understanding of how our inner and outer lives intersect, merge, yield, or sometimes come to a screeching halt and how they get back on track again.

The individuals who attend LifeWays trainings come from a variety of backgrounds and intend to apply their training to diverse activities. The typical age range is from early twenties to late sixties, and it is not unusual to find child care providers from homes or centers, parent-child program lead-

ers, nannies, parents, after-school care providers, and home-based preschool teachers all sitting in the circle of students. We also attract a number of experienced early childhood teachers who want to learn more about the living arts as a natural curriculum for being with young children. They are particularly interested in developing more skills in the domestic and nurturing activities that support practical, daily life and how to create rhythms and routines that are not overwhelming, yet are interesting and engaging.

Currently there are LifeWays trainings available in several locations in North America. These part-time trainings are comprised of on-site courses with mentor-supported independent study requirements to anchor in experience the principles and practices taught in the trainings. A complete training cycle typically occurs over one year, comprised of three or four on-site sessions with a few months in between to allow the students to digest and apply what is being learned.

The *integration of learning/independent study requirements* are primarily hands-on, skill-building activities such as learning how to prepare simple and healthy meals, how to create schedules that are not overwhelming, how to grow a simple garden, and other practical skills. These are combined with a variety of exercises to strengthen the capacity for objective observation of children and nature, including the requirement to observe in at least two different kinds of early childhood settings. The more academic-oriented requirements include a number of readings as well as the presentation of a paper or project. While most students desire to complete all of their requirements during the course of the training, others exercise the option to complete the *integration of learning* requirements within the year following the training.

The mentor component is one of the most important aspects of this training. Having a guide through ongoing phone conversations and a personal visit to a student's work setting is invaluable in helping digest all that students are learning and to assimilate such learning into real life. Parents who take the training primarily for support in their role as parents are equally blessed to have a mentor who is willing to spend time in their homes with them, similar to a life coach.

LifeWays North America is working on developing courses, seminars, and workshops for our graduates and other interested people, recognizing that

any training is only an introduction and that daily life is where the most profound learning takes place. Locations of our trainings can be found on our website, www.lifewaysnorthamerica.org, along with information about other learning opportunities such as the LifeWays Introductory Seminar that can be brought to any community.

While students in the LifeWays training are not required to have a background in early childhood, they are expected to have a strong interest in human development and children. Students also need to be open to the understanding that children are spiritual, as well as physical, beings and are to be respected as individuals with intention and purpose related to their infinitely unfolding personal biographies. The developmental picture of the child is primarily based on the research of Dr. Rudolf Steiner and supported by other contemporary early childhood research.

Perhaps the best part about the LifeWays training is the opportunity to be with a group of people who are seeking similar goals and who bring a broad base of personal experience and knowledge to share with fellow classmates. Typically the training is also laced with a fair amount of levity and humor, real soul food for the times in which we live.

Here are a few testimonial statements from LifeWays training graduates:

To me, LifeWays is embracing our journey into life's uncertainties with courage, faith, and trust; it is bringing magic in the mundane and blessing our children with our presence, our love, our laughter, and our joy.

—*Kahlil Apuzen-Ito*

It is authentic, natural living and keeping childhood kindled with magic and mystery.

—*Rebecca Fenton*

It means to stimulate my mind, to nurture my heart and to nourish my soul, and to bring joy and purpose to the children that I meet.

—*Serena Syn*

Bringing Beauty to the lives and families of young children.

—*Elisa Rios*

a warming of the heart
a strengthening of the soul
building of the community
and a promise for the future

—Kelly Stewart

A primary intention of the LifeWays training is to help the students come to a place where their own "Yes" to life resonates with and supports the children and families who come into their care.

LifeWays Membership

LifeWays North America became a membership organization in 2007 to better support those who were attracted to caring for children in this way. Members help us build our organization, maintain our website, produce our semi-annual newsletter, and develop our trainings and seminars. If you'd like to help support us in our work, there are several ways to do that.

Those who are in the *Friends* category are individuals or organizations who believe in LifeWays' mission and want to help insure that the work of the organization will continue to grow and thrive. *Friends* receive our semi-annual newsletter.

Individuals or groups who want to be associated with LifeWays on a professional membership level have three options:

Self-Affiliates are those who have not completed the LifeWays training, yet want to align themselves with the ideals of LifeWays. They are listed on our website and receive our newsletter.

Trained Affiliates are LifeWays graduates who are assimilating the principles and practices they learned in their training into their work with children and families. They receive our newsletter, are listed on our website, and can have a link posted to their own websites. They also can receive discounts at LifeWays events.

Representatives are those in homes or centers who are committed to representing LifeWays in their work and are willing to open their sites for LifeWays students to observe and learn how LifeWays principles and practices look in real life. *Representatives* receive newsletters for each family in their

care, are highlighted on our website, receive reduced tuition for any caregivers they send to LifeWays trainings, receive LifeWays consulting as needed, and can attend LifeWays events for free.

The path toward becoming a LifeWays Representative includes a self-assessment study and an assessment visit from a LifeWays board member or other LifeWays consultant. After the visit, the consultant submits a report to the Representative applicant, the LifeWays Executive Director, and other members of the membership committee. In some cases, but not typically, a request may be made for another assessment after specific changes have been implemented. Once all parties agree that the site is ready to be a LifeWays Representative, it is listed as such on the website and other outreach materials.

LifeWays is not a cookie-cutter model of early childhood care. Even within LifeWays child care centers or homes one can experience subtle differences and a wonderful variety of individuals providing the care for groups of children and families. There are, however, at least three key elements that will be found in any LifeWays Representative site:

1. Relationship-based care where children can spend a minimum of two years, and ideally more, with the same primary caregivers or teachers.

2. Living arts as the foundation of daily life activities with the children.

3. Homelike, noninstitutional environment, even if the site is within an institutional building.

If you wish to observe at a LifeWays Representative site, please call for an appointment, and please be respectful that you will be visiting children in their home away from home. Imagine, if you will, that you are walking into someone's living room (and you may be!), and don't be surprised if someone puts a broom in your hand or invites you in some other way to participate in the life of the home, like an auntie or uncle dropping by for a visit. We like to protect the children's sense of wonder and deep connection to whatever it is that they are doing, and thus ask our visitors to blend in quietly and respect the guidance of the caregivers.

To learn more about becoming a LifeWays member or about the expectations for LifeWays Representatives please check our website at www.lifeways northamerica.org or contact the central office in Norman, Oklahoma.

Perhaps the best part of being a LifeWays member is knowing that you are participating in spreading the vision that healthy living, based on strong relationships, practical and artistic activities, common sense rhythms and routines, and *joie de vivre* is a rightful and worthy approach to the care of young children and that models of such care can be found in the world!

A Word About Advocacy

Actually, I cannot write just a word about advocacy. It needs to be at least two words: "Do it!" By offering healthy care in homes, centers, parenting programs, after-school programs, and your own homes as parents, you are already advocating for children and childhood.

While having the capacity to compromise when absolutely necessary, it is also important to know when to challenge the ruling paradigm. I remember fondly when one of our youngest LifeWays students told the story of being informed that she could not clean out the rabbit hutch when the children were around. It was not a situation where the hutch was in bad shape or that unhealthy spores would be released into the air. However, she was told by her licensing agent that she could not clean it. Respectfully, she said, "Well, if I never change the rabbit hutch in front of the children, how will the children ever learn the importance of changing the rabbit hutch?" Her licensing person respected her query and gave permission for her to clean the hutch.

I know another care provider who had a beautiful nap room but was told she could not keep it because the beds were too close to one another. The escape route was clear—there was a door in the nap room; the beds were separated by private canopies to create a restful space for each child; and it was easy to move around in the space. The caregiver requested an exception twice and was rejected each time. Finally, on her third request, she was able to keep her peaceful nap room.

LifeWays worked closely with licensing in a state that does not allow mixed ages of children in child care centers. Children under two must be separated from children over two. In fact, the model most accepted is one that separates the children by age at every developmental stage. Typically there are separate rooms for infants, toddlers, twos, threes, preschool, and kinder-

garten. With respect and with guidance from a former licensing agent, we were able to obtain an exception. This meant that we could have a child under two with the older children (only six or seven children in a group), as long as we wrote up the reasons why the parents wanted the child in this group and how the child's needs would be met. An exception is not the same as an exemption, but we were happy to get it anyway. A full exemption sometimes involves working at the legislative level to get a ruling or law changed. It can be time-consuming and requires a certain amount of savvy about working with the legal system.

Perhaps the most important thing to consider is that "no" sometimes means "maybe." When we started working with this particular state licensing office, we were told from the beginning that we could NOT have children under two in our center. It was only through perseverance and respect for the legal agents with whom we were working that we finally had a breakthrough. As Mary said in her chapter on licensing and regulations, all parties involved are typically concerned about the health and well-being of children. Our job sometimes is to elucidate how we will meet the intent of the law if not the letter of the law.

Sometimes we can be advocates not only in professional early childhood settings, but in our private homes as well. The book *Free Range Kids: Giving Our Children the Freedom We Had Without Going Nuts with Worry*, by Lenore Skenazy, really caught my attention because several months earlier I had written a note to myself that someday I wanted to write a book called *Free Range Children: Organically Grown*. Little did I know that someone was ahead of me on that one! The author really advocates for a sane and loving way to raise children that is not fear-based and that allows children to explore their world.

Children in LifeWays settings are well protected—not out of fear, but out of strong relationships that have been fostered with long-term caregivers, with parents, between colleagues, and, in the best of all worlds, with the regulatory agents. If we want children to continue to be able to play creatively; explore nature; be with children of all ages; have a healthy balance between active play and quiet, restful time; have healthy, whole foods; and have a childhood that is not about becoming adults but is about being children, then developing such relationships is a very worthy endeavor.

If you are interested in advocacy, here are some suggestions:

1. Raise questions whenever possible—in a child care conference, during a licensing visit, or in a child development class, for example. Sometimes people just need to hear the existing paradigm examined, honestly and respectfully, to begin to think a different way about things (like the rabbit hutch story).

2. Write editorials, commenting on newspaper or Internet articles and blogs. Again, if done respectfully, it can make people think about how children are being raised and if there might be a different way.

3. Put out positive messages to the rest of the early childhood world about what you are doing. For example, when the Wisconsin Early Childhood Association sent out an e-mail soliciting photos for a display of early childhood programs to be viewed in the rotunda of the state capitol, Mary saw it as an opportunity—not just to get the legislators to see what we are doing at LifeWays, but to engage the conventional child care folks. She submitted beautiful photos highlighting the Forest Kindergarten and the organic gardening programs. The WECA folks were very glad to have the photos, as LifeWays provided the only nature pictures in the display.

4. Support advocacy organizations such as the Alliance for Childhood that dedicate their efforts to raising awareness about the natural developmental stages of children and the importance of having systems that appropriately support those stages.

5. Be the change you want to see. Take good care of yourself and find joy in life. People are typically more attracted to learning about your approach to life if they can see that it has an uplifting quality. Recently I heard Jane Goodall speak on the radio, and I was very moved by what she had to say about advocacy: "You will never change people by shouting at them and telling them they are bad. You need to touch their hearts."

Thank you, friends, for your interest in LifeWays. If you want to become more involved with our work, we would love to hear from you. You can reach us through our website, www.lifewaysnorthamerica.org, or by phone.

Works Cited

Chapter 1: What Is LifeWays Child Care?

Schunemann, Mary. *This is the Way We Wash-a-Day and Sing a Song with Baby,* Singing with Children series. Mill Valley, CA: Naturally You Can Sing Production, 2003.

Louv, Richard. *Last Child in the Woods: Saving Our Children from Nature-Deficit Disorder.* Chapel Hill, NC: Algonquin Books, 2005.

Zeedyk, Suzanne. *Away-Facing Strollers Research*, Dundee University's School of Psychology. London, England: National Literacy Trust, 2008.

Trimble, Stephen, and Nabhan, Gary. *The Geography of Childhood: Why Children Need Wild Spaces.* Boston, MA: Beacon Press, 1994.

Stugard, Jaimmie. Toothbrushing Song. Milwaukee, WI: LifeWays of Wisconsin, 2009.

Lamb, Michael. "Childcare stress for toddlers." *BBC News.* http://news.bbc.co.uk/pr/fr/1/hi/education/4261120.stm (2005)

Chapter 4: Home Away from Home— Rhythms, Routines, and the Living Arts

Rosenberg, Debra, and Reibstein, Larry. "Pots, Blocks, and Socks." New York, NY: *Newsweek*, Spring–Summer 1997.

Dombro, Laura, and Wallach, Leah. *The Ordinary is Extraordinary.* New York, NY: Simon & Schuster, 1988.

Finneran, Kathleen. *The Tender Land: A Family Love Story.* New York, NY: First Mariner Books, 2003.

Skenazy, Lenore. *Free-Range Kids: Giving Our Children the Freedom We Had Without Going Nuts with Worry.* Hoboken, NJ : Wiley, John & Sons, Incorporated, 2009.

Louv, Richard. *Last Child in the Woods: Saving Our Children from Nature-Deficit Disorder.* Chapel Hill, NC: Algonquin Books, 2005.

Carson, Rachel. *Silent Spring.* New York, NY: Mariner Books, 1962.

Chapter 5: Finding Your Colleagues

Baldwin Dancy, Rahima. *You are Your Child's First Teacher: What Parents Can Do With and For Their Children from Birth to Age Six.* Berkeley, CA: Celestial Arts, 2000.

Brazelton, T. Berry, and Greenspan, Stanley. *The Irreducible Needs of Children: What Every Child Must Have to Grow, Learn, and Flourish.* Cambridge, MA: Perseus Publishing, 2000.

Pittman, Teresa. "Finding Your Tribe." *Mothering.* September/October, 2000, pages 74–76.

RIE (Resources for Infant Educarers). "See How They Move" (DVD). www.rie.org, 1989.

Chapter 6: Protection: The Safety and Health of Children in Relationship-based Care

ANI. "Panicky parents breed 'cotton wool kids.'" *Oneindia.* living.oneindia.in/comment/2009/05/3139.html (12/15/08).

Cohen, Tamara. "Cotton Wool Parenting is Holding Our Children Back, Says Study." *DailyMailOnline.* www.dailymail.co.uk/news/article-1040447 (8/4/08).

Flöistrup, Helen, et.al., The PARSIFAL Study Group. "Allergic Disease and Sensitization in Steiner School Children." *The Journal of Allergy and Clinical Immunology.* January 2006, pages 59–66.

Glöckler, Michaela, and Goebel, Wolfgang. *A Guide to Child Health*, Edinburgh: Floris Books, 2003.

Hoffman, Jan. "Why Can't She Walk to School?" *The New York Times.* www.nytimes.com/2009/09/13/fashion/13kids.html (9/18/09).

Johnson, Nathaniel. "The Revolution Will Not Be Pasteurized: Inside the Raw-Milk Underground." *Harpers.org.* www.harpers.org/archive/2008/04/0081992 (9/11/08).

Michigan Television. "Where Do the Children Play?" (DVD). 2007.

Priesnitz, Wendy. "The Dangers of Antibacterial Soap." *Natural Life Magazine*. www.naturallifemagazine.com/0602/soap.htm (9/5/08).

Chapter 9: Business Questions

Spence, Jo-Ann. "Straight from the Field—Reflections on the Director's Job." *Exchange*. http://ccie.com/resources/view_article.php?article_id=5015960&page=4&keyword_id= (10/27/08).

Redleaf Press. www.redleafpress.org

Steiner, Rudolf. *The Child's Changing Consciousness*. Hudson, NY: Anthroposophic Press, 1996.

Voors, Bons, and Davy, Gudrun. *Lifeways: Working with Family Questions*. Gloucestershire, UK: Hawthorne Press, 1983.

LifeWays Forms CD

AVAILABLE FOR PURCHASE

This CD contains many of the forms that may be helpful to the person beginning a child care business, either in a home or center setting.

LifeWays child care providers have shared these forms for you to use as an example. Please check with your state and local child care agencies to make sure that any forms you use have all of the content required for your program.

Included on this CD:

LifeWays Principles and Practices
Sample Parent Handbook, center and home program
Sample Policies and Procedures, center and home program
Sample Budget
Sample Registration Forms
Sample Tuition Schedule
Sample Attendance Log
Sample Infant/Toddler Daily Log
Sample Promotional Flyers
Sample Ads
Sample Business Plan
Sample Staff Evaluation Forms
Sample Parent Newsletters
LifeWays Training Information
LifeWays Membership Structure
LifeWays Consulting and Workshop Information

The CD is available for $15 from LifeWays North America. To order, please visit www.lifewaysnorthamerica.org.

About the Authors

CYNTHIA ALDINGER (*above right*) is founder and executive director of LifeWays North America. She has lectured and presented internationally, directs trainings and seminars across the United States, and is an adjunct faculty member at Rudolf Steiner College in California. She served fourteen years on the board of the Waldorf Early Childhood Association of North America, is a member of the National Association for the Education of Young Children and a supporter of the Alliance for Childhood. A former Waldorf kindergarten teacher, Cynthia received her Waldorf teaching certificate at Emerson College in Sussex, England, and her associate business certificate from the University of Oklahoma.

A mother and grandmother, Cynthia has been married to Michael for almost forty years. Her passion is the preservation of the playful spirit of child-

hood and helping to create healthy, comfortable, and secure environments for children, families, and caregivers.

MARY O'CONNELL has been working in the field of early childhood education for fourteen years. She began her work as a parent educator and volunteer coordinator at the Family Center in Milwaukee, and quickly saw the need for quality child care. She opened her own home child care program a few years later and completed the LifeWays training. After five years in her home, she opened LifeWays Early Childhood Center in Milwaukee, Wisconsin, in 2002, followed by LifeWays Child Development Center in Hartland, Wisconsin, in 2006.

Mary serves as president of LifeWays of Wisconsin, Inc. and is a member of the LifeWays North America Board. She teaches in the Midwest LifeWays training, offers seminars and lectures on early childhood, and is a LifeWays consultant. She has a Bachelor of Business Administration degree from University of Wisconsin–Madison. Mary and her husband, Jim, have three children, Kyle (17), Ryan (16), and Kathleen (13).

Made in the USA
Charleston, SC
08 January 2014